Othello is one of Shakespeare's most theatrically striking plays. This Handbook focuses on *Othello* as a dramatic work which exploits the resources of the early modern stage and yet still challenges contemporary theatres. Exploring race and gender as performance issues throughout the study, Stuart Hampton-Reeves:

- examines the play's earliest performances and the problem of staging darkness on Shakespeare's stage
- analyses the play from a performance point of view scene by scene, line by line
- surveys key productions and films, tracing the play's move away from mainstream theatres
- draws together the latest criticism on *Othello*'s treatment of identity and sexuality.

Stuart Hampton-Reeves is Professor of Research-informed Teaching at the University of Central Lancashire, UK and a Trustee of the British Shakespeare Association. His previous publications include the volume on *Measure for Measure*, also in The Shakespeare Handbooks series.

The Shakespeare Handbooks are student-friendly introductory guides which offer a new approach to understanding Shakespeare's plays in performance. The commentary at the heart of each volume explores the play's theatrical potential, providing an experience as close as possible to seeing it in the theatre. The Handbooks also offer contextual documents, a brief history of the text and its first performances, case studies of key productions, a wide sampling of critical opinion and guidance on further reading. Ideal for students and teachers of literature and theatre, as well as actors and directors, the overall aim is to help a reader reach an independent and well-informed view of each play by imagining how it might be performed on stage.

THE SHAKESPEARE HANDBOOKS

Series Editor: John Russell Brown

PUBLISHED

FORTHCOMING

The Shakespeare Handbooks

Othello

Stuart Hampton-Reeves

palgrave
macmillan

First published 2011 by
PALGRAVE MACMILLAN

Palgrave Macmillan in the UK is an imprint of Macmillan Publishers Limited, registered in England, company number 785998, of Houndmills, Basingstoke, Hampshire RG21 6XS.

Palgrave Macmillan in the US is a division of St Martin's Press LLC, 175 Fifth Avenue, New York, NY 10010.

Palgrave Macmillan is the global academic imprint of the above companies and has companies and representatives throughout the world.

Palgrave® and Macmillan® are registered trademarks in the United States, the United Kingdom, Europe and other countries.

ISBN 978–0–230–53566–4 hardback
ISBN 978–0–230–53567–1 paperback

This book is printed on paper suitable for recycling and made from fully managed and sustained forest sources. Logging, pulping and manufacturing processes are expected to conform to the environmental regulations of the country of origin.

A catalogue record for this book is available from the British Library.

A catalog record for this book is available from the Library of Congress.

10   9   8   7   6   5   4   3   2   1
20 19 18 17 16 15 14 13 12 11

Printed in China

Contents

General Editor's Preface

The Shakespeare Handbooks provide an innovative way of studying the plays in performance. The commentaries, which are their core feature, enable a reader to envisage the words of a text unfurling in performance, involving actions and meanings not readily perceived except in rehearsal or performance. The aim is to present the plays in the environment for which they were written and to offer an experience as close as possible to an audience's progressive experience of a production.

While each book has the same range of contents, their authors have been encouraged to shape them according to their own critical and scholarly understanding and their first-hand experience of theatre practice. The various chapters are designed to complement the commentaries: the cultural context of each play is presented together with quotations from original sources; the authority of its text or texts is considered with what is known of the earliest performances; key performances and productions of its subsequent stage history are both described and compared; an account is given of influential criticism of the play and the more significant is quoted extensively. The aim in all this has been to help readers to develop their own informed and imaginative view of a play in ways that supplement the provision of standard editions and are more user-friendly than detailed stage histories or collections of criticism from diverse sources.

Further volumes are in preparation so that, within a few years, the Shakespeare Handbooks will be available for all the plays that are frequently performed and studied.

John Russell Brown

1   The Text and Early Performances

Othello is a dark play. A man is shouted out of his bed in the middle of the night to find his daughter gone, his country at war; soldiers brawl and kill each other in the dark, unable to recognise each other; lovers elope in the darkness; politicians send their best general at night to defend a country beset by invasion; a woman is murdered by her husband in a darkened bedroom, her murderer taking care to snuff out his candle before committing the deed. All the main characters are introduced at night, all die at night.

Othello's first audiences would have watched all this in broad daylight. Darkness had to be imagined on the open stage of the Globe playhouse, where the play was first staged, probably in 1604. Performances typically started at 2 p.m. so, even in the depths of winter, Brabantio's house would have been roused from sleep in bright London sunshine. The light may have dimmed as the performance came to an end, particularly in winter, when the weak sun would already have been setting when Othello crept towards Desdemona in her bed, casting a gloomy shadow over the east-facing stage and giving extra resonance to Othello's sonorous line, 'Put out the light, and then put out the light.' 5.1, which is set entirely in the dark, with characters literally lost and unable to see, could have been performed in the shadows of a winter's dusk.

Othello was played indoors when the play was performed at court in November 1604. This is the play's first recorded performance, even though it would certainly have played at the Globe prior to this. We know from the title page of *Othello*'s earliest publication that the King's Men also performed the play for their private, indoors theatre at Blackfriars. This would have been after 1609, when the King's Men started to use Blackfriars as a regular venue. There are records, too, of the company playing *Othello* on tour, and these would often also be indoor performances. Shakespeare would have had limited opportunities to exploit the interior darkness of the palaces, town halls and theatres where he and the King's Men presented the play. Rooms, halls and stages were lit with candles, which are difficult to control for staging purposes. However, the torches that Iago brings on in 5.1, and which Othello extinguishes in 5.2, would have been real, their use would have helped to vary the stage's ambience.

Shakespeare may have taken theatrical advantage of these natural shadows to produce a play that depends on the ability of night's darkness to conceal transgression and enable deception. Iago compares slander to a fire that spreads because of 'night and negligence' (1.1.79). He might also be talking about himself, for night and negligence are his two best allies in the play. Iago exploits the night to play both sides in Venice, yelling at Brabantio first and then joining Othello. In the middle of the play, Iago uses the confusions of the night to set up a drunken Cassio. He takes advantage of the darkness in the play's penultimate scene, when he kills Roderigo in the dark, and tries to kill Cassio.

When the Duke sends Othello and Desdemona to Cyprus during the night, Iago addresses the audience directly. He wants to ruin Othello and, reflecting on his general's natural trust in people, a plan suddenly hits him, a plan that he himself calls monstrous, and it will be 'hell and night' (1.3.418) which will make it happen.

The only true darkness on Shakespeare's stage was the black make-up on Othello's face. The make-up conjured the exoticism of far-away places, of unknown people with undisclosed potentials – and threats. Africans would not necessarily have been an unfamiliar sight in Shakespeare's London and recent cultural historians have found plenty of evidence to challenge the long-held notion that *Othello*'s first audiences would have had little or no experience of black faces. Some critics, among them James Walvin, have gone so far as to claim that Africans were 'an everyday sight' in London (Walvin, 1971, pp. 61–63). To these early audiences, watching Othello's face merge with the dusk, he was always 'the Moor', as if just to speak about 'the Moor' was sufficient to signify Othello and his tragedy. When Shakespeare found him, in a story by the Italian writer Cinthio, Othello had no name, he was just 'the Moor'. For much of the first act, Othello has no name in Shakespeare's version of the story either. He is 'his Moorship' (1.1.33), 'the Moor' (1.1.40) and 'the lascivious Moor' (1.1.135). He is called 'the Moor' more than ten times before, finally, in 1.3, the Duke greets him as 'valiant Othello' (l.53). Even Desdemona calls him 'the Moor' before she speaks the name 'Othello' (1.3.266). The play ends with Emilia shouting at the 'dull Moor' (5.2.256) and Lodovico granting Gratiano the 'fortunes of the Moor' (5.2.411). For those onstage, Othello is inseparable from his racial identity. Many in Shakespeare's audience shared this attitude. All references to the play, until well into the 18th century, call the play by its subtitle: 'the Moor of Venice'.

The text

The Tragedy of Othello, the Moor of Venice was published in a single volume, Quarto edition in 1622, nearly twenty years after it was first staged and six years after Shakespeare's death. The play was then included in the first anthology of Shakespeare's complete works in the 1623 'First Folio' edited by Shakespere's King's Men colleagues John Heminges and Henry Condell. Around half of Shakespeare's plays were published in Quarto or Octavo editions before the 1623 Folio. Although there were successive editions of most popular plays throughout the Jacobean period, the 1622 Quarto of *Othello* was the first new Shakespeare play to have been published since *Pericles* and *Troilus and Cressida* in 1609. As E.A.J. Honigmann points out, in his exhaustive and authoritative study of *Othello*'s texts, there must also have been four (now lost) texts which preceded these published versions (Honigmann, 1996, p. 1), which makes any attempt to privilege either of the extant texts a hazardous enterprise.

There are a number of important differences between the 1622 Quarto (Q) and the 1623 Folio (F). F is 160 lines longer than Q, and includes Desdemona's song in 4.3 (by contrast, Q contains about ten lines not in F). There are also small differences in the way that Q and F divide the acts and scenes. Perhaps of more significance to the overall impact of the play are the 50 or so oaths in Q which have been either cut or softened in F. Many editors have attributed this change to the 1606 Act of Abuses which made swearing illegal, but Honigmann points to evidence that scribes took it upon themselves to amend bad language when copying texts from the author's original papers

(p. 3). The question of how the texts relate to each other remains hotly debated. Some argue that Q represents an earlier version of the play which Shakespeare expanded upon for later performances to create the F text. Others insist that Q is a 'cut' version of F. Honigmann suspects that the truth might be a good deal messier than that (p. 13).

Any workshop class using different modern editions of *Othello* will quickly notice the impact of these differences, as all editions now conflate the Q and F version, with each editor making their own choices about which version to follow. Playing *Othello* with actors working from a different edition is a risky business, and the class will soon become entangled in thousands of textual variations. The challenge for modern editors is that both versions seem to be authoritative. There is no reason to think that one version is better or more authoritative than the other. Q is slightly shorter and is sometimes taken as an 'acting' text, though this is misleading as both versions are suitable for performance. Q is full of the kind of ripe, bawdy language we might expect from hardened soldiers. However, F's extra passages strengthen the play's theme of sexual transgression and they give a more prominent role to Emilia. The differences between the texts, though numerous, are not in themselves significant enough to deeply concern modern theatre practitioners. Any of the leading modern editions published by Arden, Cambridge, Oxford, Penguin and the Folger are reliable enough for performance, so long as everyone works from the same one. The edition that I've used for the textual commentaries is the *RSC Shakespeare* volume edited by Jonathan Bate and Eric Rasmussen, which is based mainly on F.

Modern editors have also added to the Q and F texts readings and stage directions. Two examples illustrate the problems and opportunities that this long-established practice gives to performance. In 3.3, Othello complains that:

My name, that was as fresh
As Dian's visage, is now begrimed and black
As mine own face.   (ll.427–29)

The lines do not appear at all in Q, but when Q was republished in 1630 (Q2), the lines had been changed. Instead of saying, '*My* name ... is now begrimed and black', Othello said, '*Her* name ...' (my italics). Some modern editions of the play prefer the Q2 version and change the text accordingly. From the actor's point of view, the change in pronoun is highly significant. Is Othello worried about his own reputation, or Desdemona's?

The second example is the stage direction for Emilia's second entrance in 4.2 at around l.100. Emilia has been sent to guard the door by Othello, who claims that he does not want to be disturbed while making love to Desdemona. In fact, he does not have love in mind at all, and instead rages at Desdemona, calling her a whore. In Q, Emilia enters unbidden at l.94, just after Othello says, 'What, not a whore?' She enters because she is concerned by what she can hear at the door. Othello must have said this line with sufficient force and volume to compel Emilia to disobey his orders and enter now. The F text places her entrance slightly later, at l.99, when Othello says, 'You, mistress'. In the F version, Emilia is summoned back into the room by Othello. The difference between the two texts is small for readers, but in performance the question of when Emilia enters, and why, is very significant. Does she have the courage to protect Desdemona from Othello's rages, or does she wait outside the door, hearing everything and doing nothing?

The sheer number of textual variants offers actors and directors an opportunity to develop a text that suits their own needs and interpretation. No Shakespeare text is completely stable or 'finished'. It is likely that Shakespeare himself revisited his plays when they were revived, and that the two texts represent different moments in the play's performance history. The surviving texts give actors and directors a repertoire from which they can create their own *Othello*.

Casting *Othello*

Othello's history is intimately bound up with the history of its casting. The major milestones tell their own story: the first female Desdemona in 1660, the first black Othello in 1821, the last blackface Othello in 1981. Shakespeare wrote a powerful play about a black man who falls in love with a white woman and then is persuaded, by a white man, to loath and finally murder her. The actors who work through the commentaries in this book will most likely be cast according to their gender and ethnicity for the lead roles. However, all of Shakespeare's actors were white men. Shakespeare may have seen a black man in his mind when he wrote the play, but he never saw a black man *as* Othello in the theatre, nor would he have seen a woman playing Desdemona. As staging conventions and social mores have changed, the play has shaken off these restrictions. Today, a blackface Othello and a cross-dressed Desdemona would be rare enough to attract immediate attention.

The casting of Shakespeare's plays would have worked in an entirely different way. Shakespeare would have known who would play the lead roles before he even started adapting Cinthio. Shakespeare was a player and a sharer in the King's Men, the resident playing company at the Globe in Southwark on the South Bank of London. As such, Shakespeare wrote for a group of approximately 16 actors on a regular basis. He knew their strengths and weaknesses, he knew how to write parts which would push them beyond their limits. However, he also had to work within the established politics typical of many such groups. The company had a star actor, Richard Burbage, and an established comedian, Robert Armin. Audiences expected to see their favourite actors, sometimes compelling Shakespeare to add parts simply to meet this demand. In *Othello*, the role of Othello's Servant, which is nearly always cut in modern productions, was probably created to give Armin a cameo in a play otherwise devoid of comic business. The character is even called 'Clown' in the text. Shakespeare had his palette set before he put pen to paper, and no one was better at exploiting it.

Burbage played Othello. We know this because commendatory verses written after Burbage's death referred to just a few of his most famous roles (out of hundreds that he played in his long career) and one of them was the 'grieved Moor'. This is fortunate for theatre historians, who might otherwise have puzzled over whether Burbage, as Shakespeare's lead actor, played Othello or Iago. Both are arguably lead roles, and at many points in the play's subsequent theatre history, Iago has been the part more sought after by star actors. The actor playing Othello has to play *through* Iago. For some Othellos, the only way to overcome this is to (literally) shout a lot, shattering Iago's dominance with sheer physical and vocal force. Was this also Burbage's strategy? If it was, he must have had more success than some of his descendants. The 19th-century actor Henry Irving was so frustrated with his bellowing Moor that he never played the part again. Only Laurence Olivier seems to have successfully raged enough to displace Iago as the play's centre, and even Olivier had to insist that Iago be bland and sexually impotent (see Chapter 4 for more on Olivier's interpretation of the play). The ambiguity over which of the male parts is the lead has led some actors to agree to swap parts on successive nights. The practice started with Irving, who alternated with Edwin Booth, one night playing Iago, the other night playing Othello, as if they were participating in a kind of actorly duel. We have no evidence that Shakespeare's troupe would have resorted to this. The King's Men would not have needed to, for the company had only one star player, so if Burbage played Othello, Othello was the lead part.

What did he look like? There are no pictures of Burbage's Othello, but a sitting portrait of the actor from 1600 (just before he played the part) gives us a way of picturing what this white Jacobean might have looked like as an African Moor. The portrait can be easily found through an internet image search and it is immediately arresting. His is the face of Hamlet, King Lear, Macbeth. His eyes are restless, furtive; his lip is noticeably curled, Elvis-like, with a menacing hint of rebellion. All we need to do is darken his skin complexion in a photo-editing program to see the ghost of the Othello that Shakespeare knew, that he imagined in his mind, when writing the play. This is as close as we can come to seeing what Shakespeare's Othello might have looked like, and it gives a hint of Burbage's magnetic, compelling stage presence, his ability to be both a compassionate lover and a murderous husband.

Burbage did not have computer effects to help him look the part. He used a combination of burnt cork and an oil referred to in the anonymous play *Lust's Dominion* as the 'oil of hell'. The term is not necessarily as deadly as it sounds. Actors first blacked up in medieval drama when representing devils scorched by infernal fires. The 'oil of hell' was an echo of staging practices that stretched back centuries by the time that Burbage applied such make-up to his face in 1604. He may have used gloves instead of blackening his hands; for his hair, a wig of wiry tight curls. His beard in the portrait is a reddish light brown, so he would have had to darken that as well. Other items which we now associate with Othello came later. Burbage is unlikely to have worn exotic robes or brandished a scimitar; these were all 19th-century innovations. Othello is a soldier, so Burbage most probably wore the costume of an Elizabethan general.

Iago's first actor was probably John Lowin, who was best known for playing dark, comic roles such as Bosola (the villain in John Webster's *The Duchess of Malfi*) and Falstaff (Hankey, 2005, p. 4). Lowin was a rising star in Shakespeare's company, which he had only been in for a short time when Shakespeare wrote *Othello*. If Lowin was Shakespeare's intended Iago, then Shakespeare must have had a different kind of Iago in mind to the aging, often diminutive Iago we are now used to seeing on stage. The *Dictionary of National Biography* describes Lowin as 'bulky but dignified, possessed of both power and grace'. He was, moreover, younger than Burbage. Possibly confused by Iago's role as Othello's 'ancient', most productions assume Iago is a mature and experienced soldier, rather than the 'four times seven years' (1.3.332–33) which Iago himself claims to be. Lowin was 28 in 1604, exactly the same age as Iago. As Lowin was relatively new to the King's Men, Shakespeare must have been impressed enough with his acting abilities to write such a long and difficult part for him. Iago was later performed by Joseph Taylor, whose success in the role was still remembered at the end of the 17th century.

Iago is a role which exploits a staging convention that Shakespeare and Lowin inherited from medieval drama: the ability of one or more characters to step out of the main action and address the audience. In the morality dramas which were still being staged when Shakespeare was a boy, a figure called Vice would taunt and tempt the audience. Vice was both a devil and a comic, he was a trickster figure who was able to move from the world of the play to the audience and back. The theatre historian Robert Weimann calls these different stage worlds the *locus* and the *platea* (Weimann, 1978, pp. 73–85). The *locus* describes the main action of the play, whereas the *platea* is the space between the play and the audience. Characters who inhabit this space (who may literally come forward, to the edge of the audience) have the ability to see the audience and interact with them. Weimann argues that this way of organising stage space in the medieval period underlay the way that Shakespeare and his actors exploited the resources of the Elizabethan and Jacobean stages.

Othello is an unusual play as Iago is the only character who seems to have direct access to the audience, and who is able to stand back and watch events as if he were part of them. Other characters soliloquise, but none address the audience as a real presence. Shakespeare had experimented with this device in one of his earliest hits, *Richard III*, a play that *Othello* resembles. Iago is a much less reliable narrator and confidant than Richard Gloucester. Iago directs Othello's gaze, shaping his understanding of the events that he witnesses. If Iago is such a malicious interpreter of action, what trust can the audience put in him as their guide through the play? Iago teases the audience with a number of different explanations for his behaviour, none very satisfactory (or mentioned again). Is he jealous because Othello has slept with Emilia, or is he in love with Desdemona himself, or is he put out because Cassio has been promoted over him? With no clear answers to any of these questions, the audience has no choice but to see the play through Iago's eyes. No other character (until the end of the play) understands all the elements of the story. Iago is not the only teller of stories: Othello spellbinds onstage audiences with his tales of adventure. But Iago is the only character who tells stories to the real audience, coming into the *platea* space to do so. He alone has access to the audience, he alone can shape how the audience views the play. No wonder then that the actor is frequently able to upstage the actor playing Othello.

Shakespeare wrote Desdemona for a boy player. We do not know his identity, but he may also have played the boy in *Measure for Measure*, which Shakespeare wrote at the same time as *Othello*, as both have singing parts in the fourth act. Shakespeare's company inherited the tradition of using boys to play female roles, a practice that Shakespeare was happy to poke fun at in plays like *A Midsummer Night's Dream* and *The Taming of the Shrew*, when onstage adolescents are pressed (reluctantly) into playing women. Shakespeare's heroines sometimes flirted with their real gender identity, most famously Rosalind in *As You Like It* who, in his/her epilogue to the audience, seems to admit that 'she' is not a woman at all. There is no such ambiguity with Desdemona. In 1610, Henry Jackson saw a revival of the play in Oxford by the King's Men and later wrote:

> But that Desdemona, murdered by her husband in our presence, although she always pled her case excellently, yet when killed moved us more, while stretched out on her bed she begged the spectators' pity with her very facial expression.

Jackson vividly describes the ability of the boy actor playing Desdemona to move the audience without saying anything. He uses female pronouns throughout, so for Jackson at least there was never any doubt in his mind that the boy actor perfectly represented Desdemona as a woman. This is very important, as modern cross-dressed productions by companies such as Propeller and Shakespeare's Globe tend to cast adult men in women's parts to foreground cross-dressing as a theatrical device. The boy actor who played Desdemona must have been capable of producing a much more convincing and affecting representation of femininity. Desdemona is a challenging role, her final scenes in particular require an actor to construct a complex and psychologically tense portrait of a woman facing death without knowing why, who continues to love her husband despite his violent abuse. The actor was not necessarily as young as the word 'boy' implies. The last and arguably best known boy actor to play Desdemona on the Restoration stage, Edward Kynaston, was playing female parts until his early 20s. In 1660, Desdemona was the first major stage part to be played by any English actress on the professional stage, and the boy player tradition declined rapidly after this.

The play that these actors would have received would have looked very different to the texts that modern actors consult. Shakespeare's manuscript would have been prepared by a scribe in parts with just the lines and the cues relevant to each player. A plot would have been pinned up in the tiring house with the key entrances and exits written on them as a reference point. We know little about the King's Men's rehearsal practices, but we know enough about the intense demand for new plays in the period to know that the four to six weeks of rehearsals typical of modern productions would have been a luxury. In *A Midsummer Night's Dream*, Shakespeare shows an amateur acting troupe meeting the night before a performance. They are led by Quince, who we might today describe as a director. There were no directors in the modern sense in Shakespeare's theatre, but someone must have organised the parts, cast them and, like Quince, explained the plot; even if, as Othello protests to Brabantio in 1.2, they 'should have known it/Without a prompter' (ll.97–98).

Although Shakespeare was sending up his own actors in *Dream*, they were not the bumbling amateurs depicted in films like *Shakespeare in Love*. On the contrary, the King's Men were professionals, able to quickly memorise new parts and turn them into compelling performances. Like modern jazz musicians, Jacobean actors had a repertoire to draw on, and were familiar enough with each other and their audiences to know what to do when they stepped out onto the Globe's stage. When Shakespeare presented *Othello* to the King's Men, he knew what they were capable of. He knew how to make the most of Lowin's abilities, he knew he had a boy actor capable of playing Desdemona, and he knew how to push Burbage's talents to new heights.

2 *Commentary*

Act I

Act I, scene i

1–3 The play begins with an explosion of petulant anger as two men enter in the middle of an argument, with the first speaker, Roderigo, apparently interrupting the second, Iago. Roderigo then takes Iago to task for not keeping his promises. Roderigo evidently feels that he has been let down and is letting Iago know exactly what he thinks. He points at Iago in l.2, saying 'you, of all people', and perhaps gestures at pulling at strings at l.3. We might first think that this will be a play about Roderigo, but before long it is clear that it is Iago who is manipulating Roderigo.

4–7 Iago is running after Roderigo and attempting to mollify him. Iago has been trying to interrupt Roderigo for some time, as he makes clear in l.4, because Roderigo will not listen to him. Iago insists that he is innocent. However, his sincerity gains an edge when he invites Roderigo to 'abhor me'. 'Abhor' is one of the touchstone words in the play and will be said again by other characters. Its vowels pull at the words 'Moor' and 'whore'. Evidently, it does not take much to calm Roderigo down, but he is still sulking (ll.6–7).

8–19 The first words of l.7 echo through the play: we *will* despise Iago. The speech that follows is a *tour de force* of manipulation. As we later learn, Roderigo is an easy target for Iago. This is how Iago practices: he warms up like a musician rehearsing scales. Iago and Roderigo have had discussions like this before. The speech is full of stops and starts as Iago does impressions of Cassio and Othello which both enrage and entertain Roderigo, who will enjoy hearing his enemies sent up.

20–27 Iago mocks Cassio in ll.20–27. He has to, because he is trying to solicit Roderigo's sympathy by complaining that he has been passed over for promotion. However, he goes beyond what he needs to say, and may even forget Roderigo for a moment. Whether Iago is really motivated by professional jealousy or not is beside the point. Iago hates first, then finds motives. Like the best liars, he believes what he says, and always stays as close to the truth as he can.

28–34 Iago's speech climaxes with an expression of righteous indignation. Iago can say this speech whilst making strong physical gestures to emphasise the injustice that *he* has been ignored but *Cassio* has been promoted. He concludes with a bitter joke: Iago will be, of all things, Othello's 'ancient'. He spits the word. Roderigo may even laugh, for although the position has nothing to do with Iago's age, there is a sort of absurdity to being Othello's – or anyone's – ancient. Roderigo adds a joke of his own at l.34, though it is a weak one.

35–40 Roderigo has taken the bait. Iago continues. That's what things are like in the army, he boasts, it's not what you do, it's who you know. At l.38, he turns the tables on Roderigo by asking *him* to be the judge. He wants Roderigo to put himself in Iago's place. In effect, Iago is scripting Roderigo into the part of his interlocutor. At l.40, Iago refers directly to 'the Moor'. This is the first time the word is spoken in the play. The moment can be an inconsequential one, or Iago can relish the word and pour his contempt into it as he says it.

40–57 Roderigo is still not completely convinced. If Iago feels like this, why does he work for Othello? Roderigo asks a fair question, but Iago is ready for it. He now starts on a new tack, one which is bafflingly convoluted. Roderigo will have no choice but to accept Iago's superior reasoning, because he can barely understand Iago's point.

Ll.43–45 show how nimble Iago's mind is compared to Roderigo. What can Iago mean?

Iago continues by describing and perhaps imitating the different kinds of characters who follow masters. He scorns the fawning servants who bend their knees dutifully all their lives until they are too old and are dismissed. Then, in ll.50–57, Iago presents a different kind of follower, one who is outwardly subservient but takes every opportunity to advance himself. This is the kind of servant Iago will be to Othello.

58–67   Iago again baffles Roderigo, and probably the audience too, with quick, clever turns of logic. One way to acknowledge these lines' demands on modern audiences is for Roderigo himself to look puzzled. He's not exactly the brightest of Shakespeare's characters after all. Iago's conclusion is terrifying, all the more so because it is his most honest line in the play: 'I am not what I am.' Iago is trying to reassure Roderigo that he is still on his side even if he continues to follow Othello. However, Iago's elliptical logic may disquiet Roderigo. Iago has said more than he meant to say, but fortunately Roderigo is too obsessed with his own unfulfilled ambitions to notice. Iago may even relish the risk he has taken in so brazenly telling Roderigo the truth.

68–84   Roderigo now needs no more persuading. He relishes the thought of ruining 'thicklips'. Othello has now been mentioned three times in the play, but not yet named. Roderigo and Iago are either unwilling or unable to do so, and they show their contempt for Othello by talking about him like this.

Ever an opportunist, Iago takes the moment by suddenly increasing the pace. There is no more time for sulks and argument. Now Iago speaks with a fierce urgency to rouse Roderigo into unthinking action. Every two or three words is a new instruction: do this, go there, do that.

Roderigo's original outburst was no more than a temper tantrum, and it is now forgotten as events drive both characters forward. At l.70, Iago might gesture up to Brabantio's bedroom window, which is usually placed in an above-stage space. They must now start moving across the stage towards the house, for on l.76 Roderigo announces that they've arrived. Emboldened by Iago, Roderigo gets ready to shout up to Brabantio's window.

Iago and Roderigo need to make a lot of noise to wake Brabantio and his household. As well as shouting, they can bang on doors, kick bins, rattle anything to hand in order to rouse the house. The lines here do not need to be strictly followed either, so long as Brabantio wakes up. Roderigo first attempts to rouse Brabantio are obviously weak (l.81), because Iago has to intervene (and take another risk) by screaming 'thieves'. Iago's shrill, alarming calls contrast with Roderigo's pathetic 'what ho!'

85–116 Brabantio appears above and his first lines will be pelted down to Roderigo to shut him up. It is conventional (but not compulsory) for Brabantio to wear a night shirt and hold a torch, as if he has literally just woken up from his bed. He may also be accompanied by servants.

Iago is taking a big risk in this scene, as Brabantio knows him. Iago has to hide, but he does not trust Roderigo to make a good job of enraging Brabantio, so he also has to do a lot of the work for him. Iago shouts crude insults which are both bawdy and bossy. He wants Brabantio to be angry.

The risk pays off. Brabantio does not notice Iago, and is irritated to be woken up by Roderigo, who he clearly has a very low opinion of. Brabantio now browbeats Roderigo, who simpers deferentially. Roderigo is failing to have much impact. Iago will have to intervene despite the risk that Brabantio might recognise him. But then, perhaps, Iago enjoys taking these risks?

117–54 Iago is more blunt than Roderigo. He mocks Brabantio by imagining him as the head of a family of horses. Brabantio forgets Roderigo for a moment and challenges Iago, whom he does not recognise. Iago coarsely tells Brabantio that his daughter and Othello are copulating. Cruel and crude as they are, Iago's lines are funny. Brabantio has been cuckolded.

Iago's intervention compels Brabantio to turn to Roderigo for an answer. Roderigo may be a spineless and simpering idiot, but at least he is not as blunt as Iago. Brabantio has no stomach for such direct descriptions of his daughter's behaviour.

Roderigo tells the story of Desdemona's elopement in a long, rather snivelling speech that, for the first time in the play, explains in full the incidents which have only been alluded to before. Roderigo persuades Brabantio to look for Desdemona. Iago's insults have already struck home and he has lost his earlier aggressive swagger. His instructions can be whispered weakly to servants onstage with him, or barked frantically to offstage attendants – but either way, his call for light is both a literal and metaphorical one. We are seeing a man

on the precipice of a terrible fall. Brabantio exits in a state of alarm
and shock.

155–70 Iago takes advantage of the short time he has to get away
before Brabantio comes out of the door. He talks hastily, he does not
let Roderigo reply (does he try, does Iago stop him, or is Roderigo
really *that* weak-willed?). Iago may have half-an-eye on the door,
because Brabantio might be back at any moment. At the end of this
speech, Iago runs offstage, perhaps after hearing the door opening.
The scene's momentum will be sustained best if Brabantio enters
before Iago has even managed to leave the stage, but it is also worth
experimenting to see what Roderigo will do if left onstage alone for a
moment.

171–end Brabantio enters, flustered, his lines darting back and forth
incoherently. Roderigo, whom earlier he had dismissed, he now treats
as a brother or son. Roderigo leads him offstage. The torches his
servants have brought onto the stage follow, but illuminate nothing.

Act I, scene ii

The opening reverses the dynamic of the previous scene, for now it
is Iago who enters agitated, Othello who is calm. They are outside of
Othello's house (as we learn at l.49) but we do not know why. Iago tells
Othello a wholly different version of the scene we have just witnessed
as Iago reports his earlier conversation with Roderigo.

1–5 Iago may give a little of himself away in ll.4–5. Although he
boasts that he could never murder in cold blood, he relishes describing how close he has come to stabbing Roderigo, even telling Othello
exactly how he would do it. When Iago says 'here' in l.5, he dramatises how he would thrust the dagger into Roderigo's chest. The actor
can either gesture towards his own chest, or to Othello's. This brief
moment of acting out a murder should be disquieting to the audience,
even if Othello (like Roderigo) seems oblivious to this small glimpse
of Iago's true character.

6–11 Othello has no interest in Roderigo at all. Iago carries on talking about him anyway. Iago is acting like a tell-tale, but Othello is not

a man for gossip and probably does not pay Iago much attention in these lines. Iago had hoped that his story would anger Othello, but Othello does not seem to feel at all threatened by Roderigo's actions.

11–18 Iago suddenly changes the topic of his speech to Othello's marriage. He asks Othello directly if he is married, but the text does not say what provokes this question. Possibly Othello's distracted behaviour gives the game away. He has said little, and is impervious to Roderigo's insults. Iago talks instead about Brabantio and how he will react to the news of the marriage.

Iago is trying to build a sense of approaching crisis, but Othello's mind is too full of Desdemona to care.

19–30 Othello is confident that he has nothing to fear from his new father-in-law. Let Brabantio do what he will, he says, my services to the State will protect me, all will be well. Othello's last lines suggest that Iago has been trying to persuade Othello and Desdemona to hide or escape Venice – either of which would inevitably lead to their exile and ruin. However, Othello is not a man easily influenced. Othello spots torches coming towards their party from offstage.

31–35 Iago assumes Brabantio is approaching and warns Othello that he should hide. Othello stands his ground. Ll.33–35 make an important statement about Othello's character which both echo and reverse Iago's earlier insistence that 'I am not what I am.' Othello, by contrast, says, 'Not I, I must be found.'

36–55 The torches are not Brabantio's, they are Cassio's. Othello's next lines could be addressed to Iago, but they seem better addressed to Cassio, who is clearly in a desperate hurry and so must run onstage to press Othello into the Duke's service 'even on the instant'. Cassio's business is urgent, and Othello is prepared to follow him, but instead of immediately doing so, Othello goes back into the house. He is coy about his reasons, but he goes to see Desdemona.

56–65 Othello's decision to go into his house surprises Cassio, who expected Othello to leave with him immediately. What could be more important than responding to the crisis? Iago explains first with an impenetrable piece of innuendo, then he says, simply, that Othello is married. Cassio sounds shocked, and his first question perhaps betrays the reason for his concern, because he must know the answer to his own question. Who else could Othello marry but Desdemona? This is the first hint that there might be more to Cassio's relationship with Desdemona. Although the play is clear that Desdemona never had an affair with Cassio, there is plenty of opportunity for the actors playing Desdemona and Cassio to explore their ambiguous relationship.

Iago deliberately teases Cassio by not giving him a straight answer, and he takes advantage of Othello's return to leave Cassio in suspense. The scene is moving fast now, too fast for stories or explanations.

56–73   Brabantio now enters, propelling the narrative towards its first major conflict. Brabantio, Roderigo and their men find Othello, Iago and their men. There is a brief stand-off, and as usual Iago has a plan. He beckons threateningly to Roderigo. But it is Othello who stops the fight, telling his men to put up their swords and give in to Brabantio. This is not what Iago hoped for or planned. Othello is a hard man to provoke.

74–end   Brabantio is furious and in 20 lines demands to know where his daughter is and insults Othello repeatedly. He also accuses Othello of enchanting Desdemona. And Othello just listens – stands and listens and then appears to accept his arrest with dignified composure. Of course, he can afford to, we already know that he plans to appeal to the Duke. Brabantio has no choice, but he is quick to see the opportunity to put his complaint directly to the Duke, and does not even think to ask why the Duke is in council late in the night. Othello's behaviour is as manipulative as Iago's, for although he outwardly submits to Brabantio's authority (which Brabantio, spoiling for a fight, did not expect), Othello remains in control of himself and the events around him. The text gives us nothing about Iago or Roderigo's reactions for the rest of the scene, as they have no more lines. But they will react, even if they do not outwardly show it. The full party leaves the stage together, but it is not clear who is leading whom.

Act I, scene iii

This is a key scene. The initial story set up in the two preceding scenes is unexpectedly resolved early (as the Turkish plot will also be), even if that resolution is imperfect. But the end of the story introduces the key elements of the following play: Iago's new plot (hatched but not yet revealed), the move to Cyprus and, most importantly, Desdemona herself, who finally appears onstage. The first part of the scene shows the Duke busy organising his response to the Turkish threat to Cyprus. Little of this is essential to the plot or the play, and theatre companies often cut this episode as much as possible, particularly when the cast is too small to allow for minor parts like the Senators. However, this episode serves two important roles. First, it gives actors and audiences a brief respite from the argument between Othello and Brabantio, and so shifts the point of view of the play to the Duke's. Second, Shakespeare is misdirecting the audience to think that the Turkish invasion is more important to the story than it actually is, and he capitalises on this in the following act.

In the 1622 Quarto, the stage direction places the Duke and the Senators around a table set 'with lights'. Many productions follow this direction but the table is not essential to the scene, so it is worth exploring different ways of performing this moment of crisis. The scene can be a slow, midnight discussion between grave old men, or it could be a fast-paced, business-like meeting of executives.

1–51 Confusion now overtakes the stage as Senators and their staff turn it into a war room. News is coming in about the situation in Cyprus, but rumour and truth have become entangled and no clear understanding of what is happening is yet available. The Duke is at the centre of this activity. He needs to come to a decision quickly. He does not trust the information he is being given, so he listens carefully to his advisers. The Second Senator makes a decisive point, persuading the Duke that although the reports disagree about the number of Turkish boats, all confirm the prospect of an invasion.

As new messages come in, the Duke and the Senators interpret them with an increasing sense of political realism. The story unfolds rapidly: the Turks are sailing to Rhodes, which the First Senator argues is an attempt to mask their real purpose. The Duke agrees. Another messenger brings news that the Turks have joined with a second fleet at Rhodes and are now making for Cyprus. The news that seemed so incredible at the start of the scene is now confirmed.

How much of this detail needs to be communicated to the audience? Probably very little; attentive audiences might catch the nuances of the plot, but the point of the scene is to represent a sense of the pace of the crisis, establish the Duke as a leader who listens to counsel and then judges, and heighten the sense of immediate political threat. This is a busy, tight, fast piece of theatre which does not require actors to labour over the details of a story which will be resolved without incident by the start of the following scene. The First Senator's speech (ll.22–35) is inelegant, technical and probably impenetrable to modern (and possibly early modern) audiences. Despite its detail, the speech is not designed to convey the story to the audience, but to summarise a complex political position to the Duke. Most of the detail is there to texture the scene, to give the impression of a more complex world beyond the stage. It is important to catch the political relationship between the Senators and the Duke and show the Duke responding intelligently, concisely synthesising the advice he is being given and coming to quick conclusions. The Duke says little, but every line is addressed to him, and the fate of Cyprus hinges on his decision.

52–57   The First Senator now sees Othello and Brabantio arriving. Although the Senator clearly says he sees Brabantio (and the old man is no doubt leading the party), the Duke greets only Othello, who he is anxious to discuss the Turkish threat with. The Duke is evidently so anxious to hear Othello's views that he does not listen to the Senator.

At l.55, the Duke sees Brabantio and apologises to him. Even if the Duke has made an honest mistake, will Brabantio feel snubbed? We already know that Brabantio was surprised to learn that he was not also summoned along with Othello. There is something going on here, some past history, which Shakespeare will only hint at. This leaves the actors the opportunity to find complexities and tensions in what is otherwise a very minor relationship in the play, as this is the only scene that the Duke and Brabantio have together. With that in mind, Brabantio's reply (l.57) may have an edge to it.

57–65   Brabantio is not interested in politics, instead he presents himself as a father on the edge of despair. His lines are so moving that they distract the Duke and the Senators from their military planning. When Brabantio asks for the Duke's pardon at l.57, he may be momentarily overcome with grief. Too emotional to speak, he may need support from his servants, or possibly the Duke comes over to comfort him. The Duke is concerned, and puts aside his civic duties to listen carefully to Brabantio, who begins to explain himself, but at l.61 is suddenly unable to explain what his grief is. His actions suit his words now, as he is himself engulfed by his 'sorrows'. Concerned, the Duke asks Brabantio what has happened, and all Brabantio can do his cry out 'my daughter!'

66–72 This is a shocking moment for the Duke and the Senators, who assume, with horror, that Desdemona must be dead (l.66 can be spoken by either the Duke or one of the Senators).

Brabantio's sorrow now turns to rage. His next speech is angry, violent and just as shocking as his last. Brabantio does not deny that Desdemona is dead. She is dead to him. The word 'dead' has provoked this outburst. He may look at Othello at l.69.

In ll.70–72, as he rages about Desdemona's unnatural blindness, sense and meaning break apart.

What is Othello's reaction? Othello stays silent, unprovoked even though he knows that Brabantio is using a rhetorical trick (Iago and Othello are not the only persuaders in the play) to make the Duke angry before revealing Othello as the man who stole Desdemona.

73–85 Ll.73–78 are emphatic lines, as the Duke gives Brabantio the firmest assurance he can that the culprit will be punished. The Duke is adept at moving between the political and the personal. He is more decisive and makes bolder threats than he did when receiving news of the Turkish invasion. This is, at least, a problem that he can use his authority to solve. He even boasts that he will prosecute the man even if he is the Duke's son. This is a bold promise that heartens Brabantio.

The Duke is momentarily put on the back-foot, as Brabantio identifies Othello as the man who has eloped with his daughter. The Duke and the Senators are astonished. Othello says nothing, as Brabantio notes at l.85. All eyes are on Othello, who has been quietly standing by until now.

86–104 Othello responds, not only to the Duke but to everyone there, and he commands the stage by doing so. Where Brabantio's words were formed out of anger and bitterness, Othello seeks to persuade his audience that he is innocent of the charges laid by Brabantio. He modestly apologises for his own 'rude speech', but this self-depreciation is a trick Iago would appreciate, for Othello's speech captivates the Duke and prevents him from taking hasty action. Othello talks about his physical strength, he gestures to his body and to his arms, and reminds the Duke of his active service. However, as this speech shows, Othello's real power lies in his ability to tell stories.

105–41 Othello's last words provoke Brabantio, who subverts the end of Othello's speech by completing the metrical line that Othello leaves hanging. He is incredulous, furious – how could Desdemona possibly be won by this man? Brabantio again accuses Othello of witchcraft, but his accusation is a desperate one which Othello does not rise to.

The Duke is now acting noticeably more even-handed. There is no proof of witchcraft, this needs looking into. Yet the Duke seems curiously reluctant to interrogate Othello, instead he leaves it to the First Senator to ask Othello questions.

Othello seems ready to put his case forward. Without realising the irony of his action, Othello sends Iago to get Desdemona. The rest of his lines, until Desdemona enters, will be spoken knowing that her arrival is anticipated by everyone onstage, and that Desdemona alone has the power to heal the rift with Brabantio. The Duke insists that Othello begin his story.

142–45 Othello's speech is the longest in the play so far. We have heard about Othello and Desdemona's marriage in fragments from various characters, but this is the first time that the whole narrative has been set out from start to finish. The different parts of the play suddenly come together. Othello needs to persuade both the Duke and Brabantio – and the assembled men – to acknowledge his marriage. This is the speech that Othello has been holding back until now. For the first time, we learn something about Desdemona. The play is building to an early climax with Desdemona's appearance at the end of the speech. Othello describes and in the process creates Desdemona as a character. Until now she has been a stereotype, either a virtuous daughter or a wanton, wayward woman, but in Othello's tale she emerges, at last, as a person. Few characters in Shakespeare are described with such precision – and slander – before their first appearance.

Othello's story is unexpectedly lyrical. The rhythm of his lines ebbs and flows. From a performance point of view, the listening is as important as the telling. Othello has a tough crowd: the hurt father, a judgmental executive, even (though he doesn't know it) the slighted suitor. All of them need to be charmed into accepting his innocence. He has to enchant them with words in the same way that he first attracted Desdemona. The audience too needs to be sympathetic to Othello, so it is important that Iago is offstage for this part of the scene. If Iago was onstage, he would use his special relationship with the audience to poison the moment. Instead, for the only time in the play (until the play's final lines), Othello can tell his story directly.

Othello begins by talking about Brabantio. This must surprise some onstage, not least Brabantio But perhaps Brabantio and the Senators recognise that Othello is speaking the truth. Did Brabantio once love Othello? This adds a new dimension to the relationships onstage. Brabantio has not just lost his daughter, he has also lost the man who fascinated him with his stories. Could he also be jealous of Desdemona, who has taken *his* place as the audience for Othello's tales of adventure?

146–59 We now hear a little of the stories which enchanted both Brabantio and his daughter. The Duke and his Senators must also be fascinated by Othello's speech, which even Brabantio does not interrupt (although perhaps he tries?). Othello told his life's story from his childhood until, he insists, the very moment of telling the story. This is a different side to Brabantio than the one we have seen so far. In this story, it is Brabantio who is pressing Othello for more and more stories, who cannot be satisfied by one episode in Othello's life but must know them all.

Othello continues by listing some of his adventures. Even in this briefest form, they sound extraordinary and utterly compelling. Othello speaks of floods, quarries and deserts, of wars and slavery, of cannibals and men with heads beneath their shoulders. For nearly 20 lines, Othello talks about these things, but he does not talk about Desdemona. She is absent from the speech so far. These stories have been told to her father.

Othello has a large audience, and these lines lend themselves well to a performance in which the speaker addresses the whole group, then focuses on one or two, keeping eye contact with (say) the First Senator when he mentions 'flood and field' (l.149), turning to face another Senator for the next line, and then to the Duke to tell him about his enslavement and redemption. Each part of the story is more incredible than the last, concluding with descriptions of other people and other cultures which emphasise how much of the world Othello has experienced.

159–64 Othello leaves his audience hanging on a half-line. Their appetite has been whetted, but he is not going to tell any of these stories. Instead, his perspective suddenly switches back to their telling, and to Desdemona, who finally appears in the speech at l.160. Othello can make much of the rhetorical advantage of bringing Desdemona in to the speech at this point. Ll. 159–60 are phrased in such a way that one might expect him to still be talking about Brabantio, so his audience might be surprised when Desdemona's name is mentioned instead as the person listening. Othello might also be dramatising his own surprise. He had been telling his stories and Desdemona, evidently, had been eavesdropping. She was never the intended audience, but she creeps into Othello's life in just the same way that she creeps into his telling of the story.

In ll.161–64, Othello shows Desdemona torn between her domestic duties and her desire to listen to more of Othello's adventures. The actor playing Othello can find many ways of enacting Desdemona's conflict through both his speech and his gestures. He describes Desdemona as greedy and insatiable, but within the story he remains apparently unaware of Desdemona's interest. This is the nub of Othello's answer to Brabantio's charge of witchcraft: Othello did not know that Desdemona was listening.

164–72 Othello tells his audience how he finally noticed Desdemona flitting back and forth, and decided to take the opportunity to get to know her better. In these lines, Othello seems to admit that he did use the situation to his advantage. He found a way to 'draw from her' (l.166) a plea to hear his whole story, which until now Desdemona has only heard in fragments. He then confesses that he 'did beguile her of her tears' (l.170). Othello is not completely innocent, and by owning up to his role here Othello demonstrates his honesty. When he says 'I did consent' at l.169, Othello may acknowledge that he had only consented to a request he had manipulated Desdemona to make in the first place.

172–80 Othello's story gives Desdemona a voice. Before we ever see or hear Desdemona, we hear her words as spoken by Othello. The actor will need to decide whether Othello should try and impersonate Desdemona at this point. Shakespeare uses repetition to make the speech lilting and lyrical. This is how Othello represents an adolescent girl's enthusiasm, but this is also how Othello bewitches those onstage. Othello presses on, paraphrasing rather than quoting Desdemona now, his speech approaching its next climax. He has already talked about Desdemona giving him a 'world of kisses' in thanks for the story (l.173) and now he shows how Desdemona, too, knows how to manipulate a response from someone when she says that Othello's story should be taught to anyone who wants to woo her (l.180). The line is an obvious 'come on' and Othello may offer his audience a wry smile at this point (or the audience may react knowingly).

180–84 Everything Othello had wanted to say has been said, and he has kept the attention of his audience, including Brabantio, for the course of 40 lines. All he does now is sum up his case, like a lawyer speaking for the defence. This is what happened, he says, and this is why it happened. The only witchcraft he used was his ability to tell stories, a skill which he has also demonstrated to the Duke and his Senators. Again acting like a defence lawyer, Othello' *coup de grâce* is to produce Desdemona as the witness who will end all doubts. He has timed his speech perfectly. There is no need for Brabantio to argue with him, or for the First Senator to question him further about the details of his speech. Desdemona can verify all that Othello has just said.

185–89 How does Desdemona 'witness' Othello's tale? She will shortly speak herself, but does not do so immediately, and when she does it is because Brabantio insists. There are various ways to play this, but it may be that Desdemona simply bears witness by greeting Othello, kissing him, standing with him, presenting together the image of a happily married couple. She must be nervous to see her father and the Duke.

Iago enters with Desdemona, since he has brought her from Othello's house (where she has been hiding). When he left the stage, all was going to plan, but Iago had not reckoned on Othello's ability to charm the Duke, who now confesses that such a story could have won his daughter as well. The mood onstage has changed decisively, and Iago may wonder why. The Duke turns to Brabantio and tries to persuade him to accept the situation.

190–94 Brabantio has one last chance to win his point. Ll.190–92 are angry and a little desperate. Brabantio can see that the Duke is spellbound, but he will not accept Othello's account until he hears it from Desdemona herself.

Brabantio softens his tone halfway through l.192 when he turns to Desdemona and gently asks her to put her side of the story. Desdemona might be expecting her father to be angry, but he is not – at least, not yet. Brabantio is still hoping that she will present herself as a victim. This is the last tender moment he will ever have with his daughter. He asks her to look at the assembled group and say to whom she owes obedience. The question is an odd one for modern audiences, but Brabantio is quite simply asking her to either deny his authority or Othello's. The question is a trap.

195–215 Desdemona's reply is simple and gracious. She speaks directly to Brabantio, as he is the only one now onstage who (in public at least) is still discontented. Desdemona does not apologise for eloping, yet evidently she has charmed her audience enough for no one to notice this lapse.

The scene has the feel and structure of a comedy approaching resolution, when Jack will have Jill and all will end well. Brabantio relents and gives the couple his blessing, he even joins their hands together as if re-enacting their marriage. But his bitterness breaks through all too easily, and he insults Desdemona, whom he seems to disown at the very moment he approves her marriage.

216–36 The next two speeches reflect this tension between comedy and despair. The Duke attempts to bring everyone together to resolve the conflict that has been driving the play from the outset. He wishes to make his judgment and impose his authority. This will be the last word on the matter. He has listened, now he judges. The text is set out in rhyming couplets. Shakespeare often uses this device to signal the end of a scene or play. We could be at the end of *A Midsummer Night's Dream* (another play about elopement), with the Duke having his final say before the lovers retire to consummate their marriage. Everyone listens with respect.

Brabantio's reply subverts the Duke's pronouncement, and denies the Duke his role as the authority figure who restores order. Brabantio also speaks in rhyme, jousting couplets with the Duke. His rhymes are not symbolic of happy resolution, rather he uses verse to articulate his grief, his pain.

237–44 The tone shifts from the domestic to the political (albeit briefly). We are back to the hustle and bustle of the opening. The Duke briefly describes the situation in Cyprus to Othello, and he does so in prose. The situation is too urgent for poetry, the Duke has business to do, he has made his decisions, and it is to Othello, who is no longer on trial, that he directs his speech.

245–55 Othello's reply returns to the domestic implications of his marriage, which end up taking more of the Duke's time than the Turks (perhaps to his annoyance). When Othello talks directly to the Senators, his words are noticeably more lyrical than the Duke's, whose 'stubborn and boisterous expedition' (l.244) is, in Othello's voice, 'the flinty and steel couch of war' (l.246). The Duke is to the point and plain-speaking; Othello is still seeking to persuade his audience. He accepts the commission (rather grandly) and then deferentially asks the Duke to look after Desdemona. Othello probably bows at l.251 ('bending to your state'). His reference to Desdemona's 'breeding' is an uncomfortable one, since it brings in both Brabantio's role as her father and Othello's as her lover. With one word, Othello seems to simultaneously honour and insult Brabantio, who remains silent and unacknowledged.

255–58 The Duke, perhaps annoyed to find himself adjudicating on Desdemona again, proposes the obvious solution: Desdemona should stay with her father. Brabantio refuses, clearly still bitter about the match he has only just approved. Nor does Othello seek to persuade him.

259–95 Desdemona has to be a diplomat and proposes a radical solution with far-reaching implications for the play: she should go with Othello. She begs the Duke to let her go with Othello, and in doing so we glimpse the Desdemona who eavesdropped on the stories Othello told Brabantio, the Desdemona who married Othello because she wanted to have her own adventures.

Desdemona and Othello both make speeches. So far, they have had no lines together. Desdemona has spoken to her father and to the Duke, but not to Othello. Now Desdemona talks about Othello in the third person and he does the same. She even, curiously, calls him 'the Moor', though clearly not in the same way, or with the same connotations, as Brabantio. Her speech (ll.266–77) recalls Othello's long tale. Othello's speech (ll.278–92) begins with an echo of Desdemona's concluding line. They may not speak to each other, but they speak with one voice. Othello is more grave than Desdemona, and gives his absolute assurance that his marriage will not affect his ability to fight the Turks.

The Duke is anxious to press on with State business, which is more urgent than any domestic dispute. The Duke refuses to even make a judgment: you make your own decisions, he says, perhaps brusquely. He has had enough of distractions.

296–307   Othello must leave immediately. The Duke makes final arrangements and Othello, without recognising either the irony or the danger, assigns Desdemona to Iago's care.

308–14   Before leaving, the Duke makes one last appeal to Brabantio, as if to say that despite the crisis, he hasn't forgotten what Brabantio has been going through. Brabantio refuses to answer. Instead, he speaks to Othello one final time at ll.313–14, warning him to watch out for Desdemona. This couplet resonates through the whole play and will eventually haunt Othello. It is a cutting, bitter, nasty line. Does Brabantio say it quietly to Othello, or does he say it out loud so that Desdemona also hears it? What is Othello's reaction – or, for that matter, Iago and Roderigo's, who are still onstage? Brabantio can leave with the Duke, but the logic of the scene suggests he goes his own way.

315–21   L.315 can be said either to Brabantio as he is leaving – or Othello can say it to himself or to Iago. There are many ways of playing this line, each of which subtly changes the play and the character. Could Othello even now be doubting Desdemona? Has Brabantio's point made an immediate impact? Why does Othello not respond immediately, before Brabantio leaves? And again, does Desdemona hear this exchange, as Othello talks about her in the third person?

Othello is brief with Iago and then Desdemona, whom he leads offstage to spend a final hour with. The exit is unlikely to be a tender one – they are flustered, events have turned suddenly, there is little time and much is unresolved. Othello's last line is stern and patriarchal. Desdemona says nothing in reply.

322 The stage is suddenly empty and we are returned to where we started the act. Roderigo, almost forgotten in the preceding drama, has been onstage all along, and is now at the centre again. And he is lost. How long does he wait before saying anything? Does he speak immediately; is he fiercely impetuous and desperate? Or does he pause for a moment? Is he now furtive and conspiratorial? Or is he just utterly bewildered? He is certainly impotent, for his first word, 'Iago', starts a sentence he can't end. He is at a complete loss.

323–39 Iago has lost control of events, and it seems out of character that he does not now take Roderigo in hand right away. He quickly recovers and interrupts Roderigo with a false platitude. Yet Iago seems to lack patience with Roderigo, who complains like a lovelorn teenager that he wants to drown himself (l.326). This becomes the hook for Iago to work on Roderigo again. The exchange that follows is dominated by Iago who cajoles and mocks Roderigo out of his fanciful dreams. It is a brutal scene, Roderigo is bullied and bludgeoned with words.

340–97 From a performance point of view, there's no need for the audience to follow everything that Iago says. His diatribe coalesces around a single refrain: 'put money in thy purse'. The audience does not need to keep up with Iago's quick thoughts. Dim Roderigo won't completely understand Iago either, but he will be in awe of Iago's intelligence. Iago is a man who knows about the world, and for all his sulking, Roderigo is lost without him.

We haven't seen this side of Iago before. Is he putting on an act for Roderigo's benefit, or is Iago saying what he really thinks? He succeeds in pulling Roderigo out of his suicidal mood, but we never thought Roderigo would *really* kill himself. Iago's speeches go beyond what is required to recapture Roderigo. Perhaps Iago gives some-thing of himself away here, maybe *this* is the most honest side of Iago in the play. This is Iago *enjoying* being Iago, especially his abil-ity to dominate Roderigo's thoughts, making him think about money instead of love. Iago is only partly addressing Roderigo anyway, in truth he is incensed by Othello's ability to charm the authorities with silly stories. Iago is too cynical to be taken in by Othello, but he has failed to destroy Othello and his marriage, and Iago loathes failure. He persuades Roderigo to sell all his land almost as if to prove to himself that he can still control people, for all of Iago's plans so far have gone disastrously wrong. The play should have ended here, with Othello ruined and his marriage scandalised, but it didn't. Iago has lost control of events and he takes his frustra-tion out on Roderigo, his easiest victim. Iago is not ready to give up yet.

398–end The scene ends with Iago alone onstage, ruminating on his next move. Iago starts off by boasting about his success with Roderigo, but this is nothing more than a flourish. He neither wishes to save Roderigo from suicide, nor does he have a use for him. This was practice, a demonstration of the master at work, and a reassertion of his ability to control. But Iago has no plan.

L.401 comes like a flash of lightning in the gloom and offers as clear a motive as Iago ever gives us. He hates the Moor, it's as simple as that. This speech offers one of several motives for Iago's behaviour in the play which, famously, seem to contradict each other. Does Iago really suspect Othello of cuckolding him? Does he really care? Iago is indifferent (ll.403–4) but he will use it anyway. Iago will use any fuel to fire his hatred. He hates first, then finds reasons for hating. His thoughts dance, liberated by this indifference to reason, purpose, motive. Cassio comes into his mind. Iago's thoughts follow quickly, he is making plans up as he talks. He reflects on Desdemona's ability to make men lose their dignity. This is a power which is, in its own way, both opposite and equal to Iago's ability to decieve. Iago stops mid-line, as if suddenly possessed by his own genius. A plan arrives in his mind fully-formed. He doesn't know where he gets these ideas from, he's stunned by his own brilliance. His plot is born: there is nothing that can stop him now.

Act II

Act II, scene i

The play now moves to Cyprus. The change in location also signals a change in pacing and tone. New characters, new locations and new situations are introduced, and new relationships (with Othello now the unquestioned authority onstage) formed. However, unresolved issues from the previous act fester, poisoning the island's victory celebrations. Modern theatres will often use lighting and other special effects to underline the play's abrupt change of gear. However, playing the scene with plenty of attack will be sufficient to signal that the play has literally and figuratively arrived at a new place.

1–20 The scene starts with three new characters: Montana and two unnamed Gentlemen. The Gentlemen stand in a different part of the stage, for (as Montano tells us) they are on a cape, and Montano is demanding to know what they can see. They are looking out across the Mediterranean and will most likely face the audience, who thus take the position of the tempestuous sea and its storm-tossed vessels. The lines' details matter less than their strong, active adjectives which convey in words what cannot be shown onstage: high-wrought, wind-shaked, ever-fixed. Montano does not himself go up to the cape. He lacks the courage to face the storm, so his lines are all in response to the Gentlemens' descriptions.

21–46 The Third Gentleman enters (from another part of the stage, as he can't enter from the cape . . .) with haste and good news. Although he is not named, he is clearly well known to everybody, as he is comradely and familiar with them in l.21. His entrance immediately releases the onstage tension. There is now no need to worry about the Turks, they have been repelled and the island is safe. Montano's response is brief because he is astonished. The other Gentlemen will react with both relief and incredulity, perhaps coming down from their dangerous lookout, as the Third Gentleman's extraordinary news is clearly addressed to all three 'lads'.

The story is not done yet, and events are moving rapidly. As the Third Gentleman explains, Cassio is already onshore but Othello's ship is still missing. Montano's reaction is noticeably different from his despairing opening lines. Before, Montano was panicking because the loss of Othello's fleet meant that all was lost, that the Turks would invade. Now confronted only with the possibility that Othello might be lost, Montano is calmer. He is concerned, but this is a problem he is capable of dealing with. The threat of invasion unnerved him, but he knows how to respond to this new situation. He takes the lead, starting off towards the beach to look for Othello, determined to reassert his authority and his confidence following his impotent response when faced with the Turkish invasion. These lines hint at an underlying weakness in his character. Montano is self-assured only when the structures of authority are clear; when they are destabilised by invasion, he melts into panic. Although Montano is a minor part, there is plenty in these few lines for an actor to explore. For example, he proposes to go to the seaside but does not immediately set off, for the Third Gentleman has to reinforce the command. The urgency now is for 'more arrivance' but they have no need to wait, or go to shore. Cassio enters before they have time to move.

47–65   Cassio enters in haste, dishevelled from his difficult passage across the sea. He is a refugee and he is anxious for news of Othello. His actual entrance might start during Montano's previous speech, because Cassio appears to respond to it, even if Montano is not exactly the valiant warrior Cassio takes him to be.

News comes quickly. Cassio and Montano are interrupted by shouts offstage, and a fourth Gentleman enters to tell them that everyone in the town has come out to the shore to see the Venetian ships arrive. When the Cypriots fire their guns to greet them, those onstage hesitate for a moment, still anxious even though the threat of invasion has gone. The Second Gentleman hurries offstage at Cassio's order.

66–95   They can only wait now. Cassio starts to talk about Desdemona with an enthusiasm that hints at infatuation. When he learns that Desdemona has arrived on the island, Cassio becomes very excited. His hyperbolic language echoes that of the Gentlemen looking out to the stormy seas at the start of the scene, but Cassio speaks with a different purpose, transforming the language of war and invasion into the language of beauty and sexual conquest. Cassio is so wrapped up in his thoughts that he misses his pronoun, launching midway into a sentence as if completing the Gentlemans' news. He barely answers Montano's question; instead, he offers a bizarre prayer full of erotic metaphors. As he enthuses about Othello's 'tall ship', Iago's party enters, Desdemona among them.

There is a lot of potential for comedy in this section. Shakespeare leaves Cassio and Desdemona's relationship ambiguous. We never know what Cassio's true feelings are, but in this scene he seems a little too keen to flatter her. When he describes Desdemona to Montano, he does so like an ardent lover. Cassio then flirts with Desdemona, and she seems to enjoy his attention. But is Cassio entirely innocent? Is Desdemona? These are questions never explicitly answered in the text.

Cassio risks getting too carried away when he sees Desdemona. The stage picture now becomes complex and full of intriguing tensions. The party is headed by Iago, who is protecting Desdemona, but perhaps still acknowledging his contempt to the audience; behind him is Roderigo, who will be barely able to conceal his contempt for Cassio and his infatuation with Desdemona (though he will be ignored by both); Emilia enters either with Iago (and we will learn later how odd that relationship is) or with Desdemona, who remains composed despite her ordeal. She is still waiting for news of Othello's safety.

Cassio greets her as if she were a queen when she is just the General's wife. He actually instructs those onstage to kneel to her and hail her as if she were not only royalty, but divinity as well, surrounded by the 'grace of heaven'. Some editors add a stage direction which instructs the Gentlemen to curtsy, but, given that Desdemona has no lines to acknowledge the gesture (she thanks only Cassio) it is worth exploring what happens if no one follows Cassio's order. After all, as Montano asks at l.81, what is she?

96–110 Desdemona's entrance has not lived up to Cassio's promise, and even Cassio's language is noticeably less wild than it was before. Desdemona immediately wants to know where Othello is. Cassio is unable to answer, but at that moment he hears a commotion offstage. More gunshots and shouts from the town signify that another boat has been sighted.

Cassio's behaviour is unexpectedly awkward. He cannot bring himself to play the lover with Desdemona, so instead he turns his attentions to Emilia, whom he kisses. This is bolder courtesy than that extended to Desdemona, and seems oddly insensitive to Desdemona herself. Instead of reassuring her about Othello's safety, Cassio is virtually ignoring her, whilst perhaps enacting what he would like to do.

Is a seed planted in Iago's mind now? Is Iago himself taken back by the kiss? What kind of kiss is it: a polite peck on the cheek or something bolder? Some editors put the stage direction back to near the beginning of Cassio's speech to Emilia. Strictly speaking this is justified, Cassio kisses first and then apologises to Iago, who responds with a darkly cutting remark. But theatrically, the kiss is more interestingly placed as it is here, making Cassio's prefatory warning a more territorial one, and Iago's response, perhaps made whilst they are kissing, more layered and complex.

111–30   Iago now dominates the stage, but the unvoiced reactions of others onstage, particularly Desdemona and Emilia, are at least as important. We should not forget the context of this curious, bawdy exchange in which Iago plays fool to Desdemona, and so takes the fool's licence to reveal a little of his small-minded cruelty in public. The characters have just escaped disaster; Cassio has awkwardly greeted the women; and Othello is still not confirmed to have arrived onshore.

Though Cassio remains onstage, the following scene is really about Iago, Desdemona and Emilia. It is a fascinating interlude, one rich with dramatic possibility, which can be played for laughs, or can be played in ways which emphasise the play's underlying darkness. This is the comedy version of the tragedy about to unfold, a jocular banter between friends relieved to have come through a disaster, but also a gendered triangulation of misogyny, flirtatious eroticism and rage.

Iago is funny. An audience should laugh when he says 'too much' (l.115), even if it is an uncomfortable laugh. Following Emilia's line, Iago exchanges his wife for all women, and may perhaps look for support from the men on (and even off) stage. The tight rhythm of this speech indicates a sense of artifice, but Iago's stereotyping of women is also hateful.

Then the scene takes an interesting turn. Shakespeare remembers to add an explanation for this banter – Desdemona is trying to relieve her anxiety by teasing Iago. But the curiosity of this scene is that she now asks Iago to do what Cassio was doing before she entered, and praise her. Cassio says nothing.

131–77 Iago's riddles are quick and smart – perhaps too quick for some audiences, but the point will not be lost if Desdemona reacts with mock outrage. Iago's 'fond paradoxes' are evasive; superficially they represent soldier's jokes, but they also contain within them a nastiness very apt for Iago's character.

Iago finally offers a poem that seems to head towards a flattering climax, but deliberately blows it apart in the last couplet. The women expect nothing less. They have been playing along, and their reactions are deliberately exaggerated. Iago is not a romantic lover, he is a cynical soldier, and the women seem to enjoy the way that Iago, in effect, sends up Cassio, whose earlier hyperbole and overfamiliar greeting began this exchange.

178–90 Having played the fool to be centre of attention, Iago is now suddenly pushed to the fringes of the stage, to the platea space which bridges the play-world and that of the audience. The audience's relation with the scene changes as well – before, the audience could hear everything Cassio and Desdemona said. Now, the scene switches to Iago's perspective, and everything the audience sees is mediated by him.

The actors playing Cassio and Desdemona will need to read Iago's initial aside very carefully, because it doubles up as a stage direction. They are clearly flirting, Cassio finally finding some courage to distract Desdemona – *still* waiting for news of Othello's safe arrival – with playful whispers whilst kissing her fingers. Do they withdraw from the main group, or does Iago? The latter seems more likely, though either can be played. If the couple withdraw, the potential impropriety will be greater and Iago will be saying what all onstage are thinking. But as part of the group, with Iago the malcontent watching from the sides, their behaviour is, though still unusual, part of the play that started with Cassio's original greeting. But each of Iago's words colours the action. He interprets the scene for the audience in a way which makes it impossible to view it innocently.

190–229 This curious mock-romance is interrupted suddenly by a trumpet which announces Othello's arrival. Othello greets Desdemona as his 'fair warrior' (l.194). This is an odd way to describe your lover. Cassio and Iago might initially think he was greeting them.

For the actors playing Othello and Desdemona, the following lines are straightforward. The real drama is played out behind them in the reactions of Iago, Roderigo and Cassio. How do they react to Othello's return? In the few minutes when he was still missing, there was a tantalising possibility that he might be dead, that Desdemona might be available again to court or to bawd, hence her role as queen to Iago's fool and Cassio's suitor.

Othello issues commands, and is typically self-depreciating about his oratorical skills – but for once he is right, he does prattle out of fashion, excited by the reunion, eager to enjoy peace having drowned the Turks, euphoric with victory and still-new love. His exit is meant to signal the end of the crisis with which the scene began. But Iago and Roderigo remain.

230–302   Othello's last lines puncture the happy mood with unintended irony, but only for Iago and the audience. Iago calls after them as they leave, then turns to Roderigo. The stage, which for most of the scene has been busy, is now quiet.

Iago is not standing with Roderigo, for he calls him over. Roderigo may even be leaving with the others, as a minor member of the party hanging back a little. Iago goes to work on weak Roderigo, whose eyes must be following Desdemona offstage.

Iago begins by pretending to confide a secret wrapped up in a plan. He uses the techniques of a confidence trickster, taking Roderigo one step at a time into his power. Why is Roderigo shocked? Perhaps Cassio's games before were much more innocent than Iago described them. Roderigo is too dumb to have seen any subtext anyway and is too preoccupied with unrequited love to see that Cassio might be a rival. Roderigo is not a subtle man, and he is easily overawed by those who see complexity in simple things.

Iago crafts a seductive pitch, appealing to Roderigo's reason. Roderigo is not equal to the onslaught. He struggles at first. Surely Cassio's shows of affection to Desdemona were just a friendly greeting? Even as he says this, Roderigo starts to see Cassio's behaviour in a different light. Iago undermines him so effectively that Roderigo is utterly drawn in. He is now fully convinced by Iago's poisonous interpretation of the scene that he himself had been witness to only moments before.

303–end Iago has the stage to himself again, just as he did at the end of the last scene. Iago positions himself as the play's narrator, but there has never been a narrator more unreliable than Iago. We have already seen him at work with Roderigo: now he uses the same techniques on himself and the audience.

This speech makes straightforward character analysis difficult, because Iago is not a logically constructed character made out of motives and traits. Having never really discussed his motives before, Iago now seems to let slip a couple, neither of which fits well with anything else that we know about Iago. Is he *really* in love with Desdemona? Does he *really* think Othello has cuckolded him? It is futile to look for consistency in Iago, he is not a rational character. Perhaps the best way to approach this speech is to see it as Iago's attempt to rationalise his behaviour to himself. Alternatively, he could be trying to persuade the audience that he has reasons for doing what he does, but he is being no more truthful with them than he has been with Roderigo.

He has watched, and plainly seen, how the men who dote on Desdemona can be manipulated. A pause seems justified after he says 'madness' in l.328, as these last words show how far Iago is prepared to go. He even surprises himself when he says them. His next lines suggest he is still struggling with his own mind, things are still 'confused'.

Act II, scene ii

Many productions cut the 'people following', with the Herald instead addressing the audience as 'the people'. Yet having heard so much about the people of Cyprus in the preceding scene, all anxiously looking out to sea, desperately hoping for rescue, fearful of survival, it is a shame to lose the sense of Cyprus as an island celebrating its freedom. The Herald also brings news of the Turkish fleet's complete defeat – the threat is not just postponed, but ended. The stage is set for a festival which combines victory with marriage. Is the Herald one of the people, sharing in the general sense of relief? Or is he Othello's man, and so part of the politics that mark the commencement of

Othello's rule of the island? Some productions give these lines to
Cassio.

Act II, scene iii

1–12   Though simple, the language in this scene is ironic and it is
these little moments of irony which drives the performance. Othello
and Desdemona are crossing the stage, they leave Cassio alone and in
a sense they are telling him to go away. Three is a crowd and Othello
has urgent business with Desdemona, for, we learn (perhaps surprisingly), the couple have yet to consummate their marriage. This lends
an erotic undercurrent to the scene, though Othello and Desdemona
may develop this in different ways. Whatever they do, the purpose of
their exit is clear, and Cassio is left alone.

13–45   There is a gap between Othello's exit and Iago's entrance. It
is worth exploring how long this gap can be. A longer gap will give
Cassio's part greater comic effect. Iago may notice that Cassio is looking after Desdemona because he bullies Cassio into talking about how
attractive she is. Iago is a bluff soldier, he has no time for love. Every
time Cassio talks romantically about Desdemona, Iago undercuts
Cassio's sentiment with a down-to-earth, ribald comment. They play
at this for a few moments, and Iago wins every time. Cassio sounds
full of unrequited love at l.26, and Iago suggests a manly solution: let's
get drunk.

Cassio is not as easy to manipulate as Roderigo was, and he is not
ashamed to admit that he cannot take his drink. In fact, he tells us, he
is already a little drunk (l.37). Iago insists, and Cassio starts to waver.
There must be noises offstage, because Iago hears that his party has
arrived. Cassio agrees to let them in and join in the celebrations, but
he still has his misgivings.

46–61   Iago plots in the moment and enjoys taking risks. Here, he is
witty and full of light touches which allow him to breathlessly *enjoy*
his role as the play's vice-figure. His words are propelled by allit-
erations such as 'potations pottle-deep' and 'fluster'd with flowing
cups' that are anchored around the speech's first crucial word: 'if'.
The rhythm contrasts completely with the crafted, balanced lines he
spoke to Desdemona when playing the fool, or the bawdy prose just

spoken to Cassio. This is Iago naked: he is speaking as he thinks. He stops only when he sees Cassio and the others returning.

62–118 The following section, a soldiers' victory party, is short (only 50 lines) but is often staged elaborately. This post-liberation booze-up offers plenty of opportunity for boisterous improvisation. The other actors in the party can join in the songs and will egg Cassio on as he drinks back his wine and becomes more and more inebriated.

Cassio is under pressure to join in the celebrations. Montano insists that Cassio take some wine when he enters. Iago has his own reasons for getting Casso drunk and so calls for wine three times. Iago is careful not to get drunk himself (although Iago may be better able to cope with alcohol than Cassio) and he stays sober as those about him enjoy their freedom.

We know Cassio is intoxicated when he repeats the phrase 'fore heaven' three times. This is not a phrase Cassio uses again. The more that Cassio insists that he is not drunk, the more drunk he should appear. When he says he can stand and speak well enough, he should do neither. He is clearly more dissolute than anybody else. Some onstage may find it amusing to see Cassio like this, especially as Cassio is someone in authority, but Montano is concerned about his behaviour.

119–45 Montano and Iago should be establishing the watch, but Iago instead starts to gossip about Cassio. Iago is careful not to name Cassio. He picks at doubts that Montano already has, and persuades the soldier that Cassio has a drink problem. Montano clearly does not know Cassio well, as he has to ask if Cassio is 'often thus?' Iago establishes a false mental picture of Cassio and behaves as if he is letting Montano in on a long-held secret worry. Iago cleverly manages to open up a chink of doubt about Othello's judgment as well. He is clearly prompting Montano to some action, and Montano suggests a way forward himself at ll.117–18.

Including Iago's aside to Roderigo whilst Montano is speaking will be a challenge and one worth playing through in a number of different ways. Montano is so easily gulled that there is no harm in playing a little to the scene's absurdity. Iago is so sure of his own ability to manipulate Montano and Roderigo that he does both at the same time, like a virtuoso playing two instruments at once.

Ll.131–42 are, for Montano, one uninterrupted speech. He does not notice Roderigo's entrance. Curiously, l.135 ends with a direct question to Iago, making it hard for Iago to then speak an aside to Roderigo. Montano does not seem to mind getting an answer, so the question is partly rhetorical, but it is addressed to Iago. Iago will also be careful not to be seen with Roderigo, he will not want to be implicated in the fight that is to follow. Iago's lines can overlap with Montano's in performance, since Montano is at this point wittering on about Othello, apparently absorbed in his own sense of responsibility. He needs no more conditioning from Iago. The sequence of lines and entrances in the text do not need to be strictly observed. Roderigo can enter earlier and try to get Iago's attention, for example.

Iago speaks quickly (and impatiently) to Roderigo before turning back to Montano as if he had been listening to him all along. Iago now rejects Montano's plan to tell the Moor about Cassio's drinking – the very idea that Iago has planted in Montano's mind only a few lines before. He says this expecting a commotion any minute. Iago manages to present himself as Cassio's best supporter, but also allows Montano to think his own views are absolutely right. They are interrupted by a commotion.

146–64   Cassio runs in with his sword already drawn and Montano steps in his way (Iago tells us all this later).

His work done, Iago lets Montano take charge. Montano hardly notices Roderigo, instead he stops Cassio and demands to know what he is up to. Cassio is too angry to be stopped and he strikes Roderigo, but he then lashes out at Montano. Because Iago has conditioned Montano to think of Cassio as a man with a drinking problem, Montano assumes Cassio is to blame for the row and starts a fight of his own when he criticises Cassio for being drunk.

Iago at first does nothing. He is happy to let the scene unfold. He then makes a show of trying to intervene, but deliberately avoids doing anything to assert his own authority to defuse the situation. Instead, he discreetly helps Roderigo to slip away. The bell adds to the sense of alarm onstage.

165–79   The fight has drawn Othello out and his attendants quickly restrain Montano and Cassio. Othello has reason to be annoyed. He has been dragged from his marriage bed, possibly before the marriage was consummated.

Montano is hard to restrain and still tries to lunge at Cassio. He is also bleeding, but is likely to be exaggerating when he says that he has been mortally wounded. He certainly seems active enough, and no one seems overly concerned about his injuries.

Othello tries to impose his authority, but it is Iago (showing a more commanding presence than he did earlier) who stops the fight, reminding Montano and Cassio of their place – and of Othello's. Othello backs Iago up, threatening to kill anyone who 'stirs'.

179–89 The bell that started at l.161, whose 'dreadful' sound may well overwhelm all other noises, will cease around l.180 a few moments after Othello calls for it to be stopped. With the bell quieted, the crisis is over, and all that remains is for Othello to find out what happened.

Othello turns to Iago, who looks 'dead' with grieving, who started everything but seems to Othello the most innocent, the most concerned, the most devastated by the events he has been witness to (and author of). Yet Iago refuses to speak, and instead pretends to be disorientated by the fight. He cannot tell, everything was peaceful, we were about to go to bed, and then the fight broke out from nowhere, and all is blood and confusion.

190–206 With no straight answer from Iago, Othello tries Cassio, who cannot speak, and is probably looking defeated and ashamed. Othello is direct with Cassio, respectful with Montano, even though Othello calls him a 'night brawler'.

Montano again complains about his wound, and may protest too much. Montano will not say what happened though and refers Othello back to Iago.

207–23 Othello's next speech reveals his irritation. Why does no one answer his questions directly? Iago pretends to duck responsibility, but Othello puts him on the spot and so does Montano, who reminds Iago (who is of course Cassio's greatest admirer) of his duty. To everyone onstage, Iago will look under pressure to tell the truth even though it will condemn Cassio. The scene's focus is on Iago, and it is Iago who has the power to determine what happens next. Iago's brilliant manipulation of events has succeeded.

224–54   Iago goes into more detail than required, and tells his story with a vividness that only makes things worse for Cassio. Iago means this strategy, this manipulation, to be transparent and Othello sees straight through it. He is meant to. He even comforts Iago for trying to portray Cassio in a better light. On l.254 Othello is direct: without anger, or elaboration, he sacks Cassio, and neither Cassio nor Montano say anything in reply.

255–64   Is Cassio silent because he is ashamed, exhausted, still drunk, stunned by his dismissal? Or is he silent because Desdemona comes onto the stage to see what is going on? Desdemona's entrance makes Othello even angrier. He threatens to make an example of Cassio and then leads Desdemona back to bed, leaving orders for Montano to be taken care of and for the city to be calmed after the brawl. The stage empties, except for Iago and Cassio.

265–318   Cassio must look like he is suddenly struck with pain, perhaps by withdrawing or simply moaning after Othello has gone. Whatever he does, it is enough to give Iago a pretext to stay behind and show his concern for Cassio's health. However, Cassio's injuries are not physical, it is the damage to his reputation that he complains about. It is difficult to feel much sympathy for Cassio as he sobs about his drunkenness and his loss of standing.

Iago says what any friend in this situation might say. He tells Cassio to buck up, to stop behaving like a child and be more like a man. However, Cassio is incapable of stoic forbearance and instead indulges in self-pity. The remains of the night's party will still be around him – goblets, bottles of wine – and the actor can experiment with using or looking at them, as if he is surrounded by the objects which earlier seduced and now torment him. He refuses to ask Othello for his job back, he rightly senses that he would be rejected.

319–41   Iago has a more appealing plan – why not go to Desdemona? Surely Desdemona is really in charge of the General? Othello would not refuse a request from his own wife. Cassio's self-pity suddenly turns to a sort of eager desperation; he is taken with the idea, and rallies quickly (perhaps too quickly). He leaves the stage thinking of nothing else.

342–68 Iago's next speech is a brilliant example of direct address. Who is it that says Iago plays the villain? The audience, perhaps, watching the preceding scene from Iago's point of view, privy to the way he twisted the situation to his own advantage? Iago's argument is hard to disagree with. Everything he has said has been reasonable, honest. Is this a defence or an apology – or neither? Surely Iago is not being wholly serious here, as he briefly turns his tricks on *us* and tries to gull us with the same persuasive rhetoric we have already seen him use on Roderigo, Montano and Cassio. For a moment he almost has us – but he has his tongue in his cheek and, at l.356, abandons this playful audience-baiting to think once more about his next move.

Iago is making his plans up as he goes along. He can see what he needs to do and say to create the most opportune situations, but he does not necessarily have a thought-out plan. He works by instinct and seizes on opportunities spontaneously. Cassio is disgraced and will appeal to Desdemona for help. How can Iago best exploit Cassio's infatuation with her to drive Othello mad?

369–88 Roderigo briefly interrupts Iago's thinking. Iago hardly needs him now, and Roderigo is so easy to direct that Iago does not waste his talents on him. Roderigo has lost all his money, he is dejected and he wants to go home. Iago deals with him briefly by telling him to go away and stop complaining. Iago can afford to do this and Roderigo is so weak-willed and stupid that he neither protests nor complains, but slinks off as he has been told to.

389–end Roderigo's interruption seems to have crystallised Iago's thoughts, however, as he now sees clearly the next steps. Iago realises that he will need his wife to help him create a situation where Othello believes himself betrayed.

Act III

Scenes 1 and 2 are often cut in performance because they are not central to the play's story. The only real advantage to retaining them is

that they give the actors playing Iago and Othello the opportunity to
rest before 2.3 and 3.3, both of which will be demanding scenes for
both actors and the audience. The actors have the challenge of changing Othello from the successful honeymooner at the start of 2.3 to
the furious, obsessive and murderous lover we see at the end of 3.3.
3.1 and 3.2 help to make this transition more convincing, as we first
learn that Othello and Desdemona have spent the morning arguing
about Cassio (3.1) and then we see Othello about his business and no
doubt reflecting on the previous night's events. The clown also offers
the audience a moment of light relief in an otherwise grim tragedy.
However, most modern productions call the interval at the end of 3.3,
so 3.1 and 3.2's interlude from the main story is no longer needed.

Act III, scene i

1–28 Cassio has not slept and probably has a terrible hangover. He
is also completely desperate and has brought musicians with him to
wake up Othello. They start up and evidently make a racket, for the
'clown' (one of Othello's servants) pays them to stop and then accepts
a small bribe from Cassio to bring Emilia out to him.

29–end Iago and Cassio's brief exchange adds little to the story,
except that Cassio gives Iago the opportunity he has been looking for
to involve his wife in the plot – and once more it is Iago's honesty and
plain-dealing which drives the action. Emilia gives us a glimpse of the
discussions Othello and Desdemona have had about Cassio – and a
sense of the rift that Cassio's disgrace has opened up in the marriage.
This is the first hint of any kind of argument between them.

Act III, scene ii

In this brief scene, Iago keeps his promise to make sure that Othello
is out of the way. Othello is business-like, focused on the task in
hand, and noticeably says nothing about Cassio or his arguments
with Desdemona.

Act III, scene iii

1–14 Where do Desdemona, Cassio and Emilia enter from? We
have found them at the end of the meeting promised in 3.1.

A modern theatre can use lighting to discover them already onstage. In Shakespeare's theatre, they would have to enter through one of the rear doors, which have already been established earlier in the play as the doors to Othello's Cyprus home. Desdemona is showing Cassio to the door, making promises to him as he goes. Cassio will be anxious that Othello could return any minute – and he does, for Cassio sees him walking back towards the house and, despite Desdemona's attempts to persuade him to stay and face Othello, he slips away. Cassio's behaviour only makes it easier for Iago to create suspicion about his relationship with Desdemona.

Desdemona is polite, even a little formal. She has a grace and authority that we have seen before only in the Duke and Othello. Perhaps Desdemona is even imitating them, but despite her youth, she has a natural authority and plays the part of the General's wife well – even if we suspect she may be over-promising.

15–36 Cassio is deferential until l.15 when the scene changes for both of them. Cassio cannot resist a self-pitying lament. Desdemona's reply goes beyond her earlier professional manner. She makes an extraordinary promise to use all her resources to persuade Othello, even refusing to sleep with him. Together with her suggestive promise to 'intermingle' Cassio with everything that Othello does, this adds an unexpectedly erotic tone to the exchange. Cassio may notice, and Iago will certainly be quick to tug at this thread.

Cassio leaves the stage quickly, but he is spotted by Othello and Iago. How does he leave the stage? Iago describes his behaviour as 'guilty-like' and no doubt there is something furtive about Cassio's exit. His exit will be to the opposite side of the stage and Othello should just catch a glimpse of him.

37–55 The focus of the scene now briefly moves to Othello and Iago. Iago's first line is only superficially to himself – Othello is meant to hear it to arouse his suspicions.

The logic of the lines suggests that Desdemona now walks over to Othello and Iago, although she may have been waiting for them to come to her. There is something a little presumptuous about Desdemona's behaviour, especially when she immediately starts talking about Cassio. Othello surely *knows* who she means when she talks about a 'man' but he pushes Desdemona to say Cassio's name anyway.

Once again, Desdemona slips unknowingly into a semi-sexualised language by describing Cassio as a 'suitor'.

56–66 Othello is abrupt, his answers curt, laden with impatience and suspicion. Desdemona tries but gets nowhere, her first elegant appeal soon replaced with a childish petulant, demand to know when Othello will forgive Cassio.

67–82 Desdemona sets off at l.67 with a bossy, meandering speech which is perhaps meant to endear Othello to her. However, she takes an unknowing risk when she also reminds Othello that Cassio used to come with him when he was first courting her. Desdemona tries to wear Othello down with persistent questions. Othello's behaviour will partially explain the way Desdemona presses him with questions in the speech. Does he try to ignore her, is she deliberately trying to annoy him? Or does he keep attempting to answer, in a manner that Desdemona will already know is designed to fob her off? Desdemona will not be told. Her speech is a little childish, she acts like an adolescent pestering an adult.

83–95 Othello gives in to Desdemona. L.83 can be read in a number of different ways. There is enough in Desdemona's pleas for Cassio to irritate him and even plant seeds of suspicion which Iago will later cultivate. However, Desdemona knows how to get her way with Othello and when he concedes, there may be an element of (sexual?) game playing.

Desdemona immediately recognises l.84 as an implied insult and retorts with a much stronger speech. There is room for a pause here, as Desdemona has clearly bested Othello and put him in his place. All Othello can do is to repeat himself and ask to be left alone.

96–9 Their parting is awkward, they do not behave now like young newly-weds but like an old married couple after an argument. There is a distinct sourness in the air, albeit tempered by Othello's ungracious promise to come to her straightaway. Desdemona's parting promise to be 'obedient' seems to be a concession, an admission that she had gone too far – further than she expected she would have to – in standing up to Othello.

What is Iago doing during this exchange? He may well be interested to learn that Cassio helped to woo Desdemona.

100–2 The following section between Iago and Othello is one of the most challenging dialogues in the play. Iago seizes on Cassio's past involvement in Othello and Desdemona's relationship and tugs at a thread of doubt in Othello's mind. Iago pretends to be reluctant to say exactly what he thinks, which maddens Othello and yet makes Iago seem all the more honest. What Iago does not say is more important than his actual words.

Othello is already part of the way there. His first lines here suggest a depth and darkness to his feelings for Desdemona which we have not previously seen. Does he say these lines to Desdemona, calling after her? Why does he not say this to Desdemona when she is there? He talks as if trapped by love. He could begin by asking the question, 'if Desdemona does not love me' but instead he uses a more curious phrase: 'when I love thee not'. What does it mean to say chaos will come 'again'? There are no direct answers to these questions in the text, but the lines hint at darker emotions and thoughts than we've so far seen in him.

103–20 Iago may not hear these lines. Instead he takes a big risk by teasing Othello with bold innuendo. Iago is completely disingenuous. He has just heard Desdemona herself say that Cassio helped woo her, and why now call him by his full name, Michael Cassio, as if a casual thought had just struck him? Iago's single lines are contradicted by his actions – as Othello tells us in the next speech, Iago frowns, thinks deeply, says little but shows his concern.

121–42 This maddens Othello, as Iago hoped, and Othello loses his temper at l.121. He demands to know Iago's thoughts. Othello is smart enough to recognise all this as a *trick* – he either does not believe, or does not want to believe, that Iago would use the devices of a 'false disloyal knave'.

Note here that the Othello-Iago exchange is an almost exact reversal of the Othello-Desdemona exchange that preceded it, with Othello behaving as Desdemona earlier did, petulantly demanding that Iago speak, and Iago stalling with a line (l.132) similar to Othello's earlier brooding retorts.

Iago again uses Cassio's full name, and again swears he is honest, but this time there is clearly more to be said, and Iago risks drawing out the punch line.

143–48   Othello agrees that Cassio is honest, but doubt and anger are already making him doubt his own words. He sounds troubled. Iago plays with him for a couple of lines by pushing at this question of Cassio's honesty. At l.148, Othello has had enough and demands to know what Iago really thinks.

149–63   Othello gives licence to Iago to use the 'worst of words'. By keeping Othello hanging on like this, letting his orders and entreaties grow darker and more desperate, Iago achieves more than he ever could have done with simple speculation.

Iago gives a hint of what he really thinks in ll.152–60, when he admits that he has thoughts 'vile and false'. He says this to keep Othello dangling on the hook. The register of the exchange has changed. Even though Iago has already admitted having his suspicions about Cassio, he asks Othello's permission to say what they are. Earlier, Othello would have dismissed these slanders, now he will not be satisfied unless Iago tells him everything. Othello reassures Iago, and presents himself as Iago's friend rather than his General. Friends tell each other the truth no matter how difficult it is to hear.

164–82   The scene again seems to be building to the moment when Iago will say exactly what he thinks of Cassio, but once again he frustrates Othello by refusing to slander his friend. The scene's rhythm is maddening. Iago will start to talk, but then find another way of evading the topic. And that is all he says in the next two speeches: different kinds of nothing, different ways of evading Othello's questions, different ways of slandering Cassio without ever actually saying anything. Iago hides behind honour and honesty, he never says what he means, but he still manages to convey exactly what he means through allusion, innuendo and silence.

183–86   Othello tries again by ordering Iago to talk, but his Ancient will not be drawn. L.186 can be played in many different ways, as threat, frustration, anger, desperation, even perhaps a recognition that he does not need to ask any more because Iago's stubborn refusal tells its own story. Whatever Othello means, clearly the game is over. Iago has said nothing, which must mean he is hiding a terrible secret about Cassio and Desdemona. Othello's thoughts run ahead of Iago.

187–215 Iago pleads with Othello to be wary of jealousy. The dynamic of the scene has shifted, now Iago drives the scene and it is Othello who refuses to listen. Why is Iago talking about jealousy? Why the warning? Because what he wants to say will provoke Othello. Iago is looking for permission to say something terrible, he needs the licence to say what he wants to say. Othello gives it to him: he does not want to be jealous, he would need proof anyway before he could ever doubt Desdemona. This is the first time that the hidden subject of the scene – Desdemona's infidelity – has come close to being spoken out loud. Tellingly, Othello is the first to suggest that there might be cause to doubt her faith. Even though he immediately dismisses the thought, Othello assumes that is the topic of their discussion. Iago has not once directly said anything at all about Desdemona. She chose *me*, Othello insists, she had eyes and she chose me. There is no jealousy in this – and if there is proof, then there is no more love, and without love, no jealousy.

216–39 With Othello's permission to go further, Iago takes his biggest risk, and tells Othello to look again at Desdemona. Can he trust her? She betrayed her father after all. Brabantio's parting warning from Act I is suddenly remembered. It did not strike home then, perhaps it does not now, but here is the thread of doubt that Iago has been looking for. If she could deceive her father, why not her husband? Can such a woman be trusted?

240–54 What impact does this have on Othello? He should be angry, either at Desdemona or Iago, but he is not. He thanks Iago, but he says little. He is bewildered perhaps, he is confused, his spirits are 'dashed', he is 'moved'. Shakespeare only gives us hints here at what Othello will be doing and thinking. Othello's short lines should be loaded with what is not being said. Othello is shaken, exhausted, his own doubts finally said by someone else, someone he trusts.

255–67 Iago pretends to try and reassure him, to say it is only suspicion, but Othello is saying little. Iago does not want him to say anything, he *wants* Othello to stay immersed in these paranoid fantasies. As soon as Othello starts to speak and reason for himself (l.256), Iago interrupts and puts his own thoughts in, with words designed to slander Desdemona: 'rank', 'foul', 'unnatural'. Even though Iago does not speak directly about Desdemona (he even assures Othello she cannot possibly be like that) these are words aimed at deepening Othello's suspicions.

268–71 Who does Othello say 'farewell' to? (l.268). Superficially, it is to Iago, although Iago is not going yet, and Othello does not ask him to go until l.270. Is he also saying farewell to Desdemona, to love, to the conversation? Othello has said little in response to Iago and now asks to be left alone – but he instructs Iago to have Emilia spy on Desdemona. Iago has succeeded and starts to go.

272–73 Othello's first couplet is meant to be an aside, but no doubt Iago is watching. Iago has done his job well, he has got Othello hooked on suspicions that have no substance to them. Othello is convinced that Iago has more to tell him.

274–87 Iago returns as if unable to leave Othello like this. He tries to persuade Othello not to dwell on what Desdemona might have done, but this (as Iago intends) only makes Othello even more frightened. Iago is carefully conditioning Othello, bringing him to a pitch of paranoia, so that anything that Desdemona does will look like the proof that Othello seeks to give substance to his fantasies. Iago leaves Othello with much to think about.

288–309 We now learn how effective Iago has been. Othello seems utterly convinced that he has been deceived, that 'she's gone'. This speech is fragmented, reflecting Othello's own disordered mind. He jumps from Iago to what he might do if . . . if . . . . He prides himself on not being able to speak well, he worries that he is too old, but then his thoughts grind into the absoluteness of l.284: she's gone, I am abused. Where does this thought come from? Not from the lines, but from something inside, a thought that has gnawed its way through sense and logic to the forefront of Othello's mind. He dwells on this a bit more, on women's appetites, on his own destiny, on death – before spotting Desdemona approaching. This restores Othello to his senses: he'll not believe she's false, not yet, he tells himself. But he already does.

310–22 Desdemona and Emilia enter, and it seems that for Desdemona, the earlier argument is forgotten, as is her promise to Cassio to intermingle everything with his suit. Instead, she is a caring and dutiful wife who is, for the first time, worried about Othello. She has come because he is due to attend a dinner with the Cypriots. Othello is withdrawn and speaks softly. When he says he is to blame (l.313) he is talking both to Desdemona and to himself. He lies to her, claiming a headache, and rebuffs her when she tries to wipe his forehead with her handkerchief. Ironically, Othello causes her to drop the handkerchief, which he dismisses as a 'napkin'. He goes back into his house, Desdemona following looking puzzled and worried.

323–32 Emilia is alone onstage for a brief moment. Does Emilia address the audience or is she just talking to herself? Even though her lines are mainly expository, this speech gives the actor the opportunity to develop the character in readiness for the next act. Emilia faces divided loyalties. She knows how much the handkerchief means to both Desdemona, who cherishes it, and Othello. She knows (and only she knows) that Iago is 'wayward', but she does not know why he wants Desdemona's handkerchief. She chooses to give the handkerchief to Iago. In effect, she steals her mistresses' love token, a betrayal which will have far-reaching consequences in the play. These complexities of plot and character, never resolved by Shakespeare, can be explored onstage, or they can be left ambiguous.

333–56 When Iago enters, he acts like a bully, chiding his wife for being alone. She tries to tease him with the handkerchief, but Iago has no respect for Emilia at all, snatching it from her as soon as she shows it to him. If Emilia had hoped to win Iago's attention, she is disappointed, as Iago is more interested in the handkerchief. She even tries to take it back from him (maybe literally, Iago pulling it out of her way) but Iago is not going to give it up. Instead, he orders her to leave him alone.

357–69 Iago plots quickly. He does not at this point realise how important the handkerchief will be, but he suspects it will be useful.

Here, as elsewhere, we see Iago plotting in the moment, responding to opportunity and circumstances. He sees Othello coming towards him and shows off by talking directly and honestly to Othello – but only the audience can hear what he says.

370–96   Othello is ranting and hardly aware of Iago, who can only make brief interjections in the following 40 lines. Othello may not even hear Iago's comments. Othello's first question (l.350) is addressed to the absent Desdemona. He becomes violent when Iago tries to stop him talking to the air. Othello carries on, lurching from self-pity to despair to hatred. He is tortured by what he knows. He was happy in his ignorance; he is ruined in his suspicions. Picking up his earlier, ambiguous 'farewell', Othello now says farewell to everything. In losing (as he thinks) Desdemona, he also loses his identity, his dignity, his sense of self. Chaos has come again.

397–412   Othello turns suddenly on Iago. He demands proof. This is not the demand of a friend, as before, or of a jealous lover, but of a furious General. Iago is told to find visual evidence or else. Othello's attitude to Iago has changed and we see for the first time how much Iago has risked to get this far. Othello is on the edge.

413–52   With Othello lashing out in every direction, Iago has lost control of the situation. He restores his grip on Othello by threatening to leave. Othello is too far gone to be left alone in his madness and he insists that Iago stay, that there is no harm in him being honest. Anger is slipping into despair and confusion, Othello does not know who is honest and who is not, and repeats his need for proof. He needs something solid to hang on to, something real. Iago can now pretend to agree to help Othello find that proof. They are comrades, friends, again. Iago says that it is 'impossible' for him to see Desdemona and Cassio together, but if that is what Othello wants, that is what he shall have.

453–68   Iago continues to pretend to regret having been the person to arouse Othello's suspicions. But Othello wants proof, so Iago tells an extraordinary story: he shared a bed with Cassio, Cassio in the night dreamt he was with Desdemona, and then kissed and fondled

Iago as if Iago were Desdemona. This is a bizarre kind of proof and Iago may well feign some embarrassment in telling it. The story is also funny, its absurdity working as a brief counter-point (and comment on) Othello's madness.

469–74   Othello is so wrapped up in his obsessions that he does not question Iago's story, instead he sees in it even more than is there. He recoils in horror at Iago's story. Iago briefly tries to pull Othello back. Cassio was only dreaming, he points out. But this is a ruse. Othello will take any evidence as proof, no matter how thin. At ll.471–72, Othello turns it over in his mind. He is not raging, he is trying to make sense of what he has just heard. Maybe it was just a dream? Sensing that Othello is straying too far, Iago muddies Othello's mind with a further thought, that Cassio's dream adds to all the other proofs (what proofs?).

475–86   This is all Othello needs to burst into another violent fury. L.475 is significant, for this is the first time that Othello has threatened to kill Desdemona. His threat also seems wild because Othello wants to punish Desdemona for Cassio's dream.

Othello is so angry he wants to kill Desdemona immediately, but Iago stops him (l.476). Iago has to. Othello cannot be controlled if he is in a blind fury, and Iago is obsessed with controlling people. Also, if Othello leaves now, he might still return to his senses when he calms down. Instead, Iago plays with Othello, calming him down when he is angry but then throwing titbits of suspicion to keep Othello at his heel.

Iago innocently mentions the handkerchief, he does not know what it is . . . but he has seen Cassio with it. This shakes Othello, and Iago persuades him to agree to a kind of contract – if Othello sees Cassio with the handkerchief, that will be his 'ocular' proof.

487–99   Proof is now only a formality. Othello loses himself again, rages against Cassio, wishes he could kill him 40,000 times. Iago tries to stop him again but Othello just raves now – blood, blood, blood! At l.499 Othello seems to settle, his speech becomes more ordered, less random and violent. He will never now change his mind. He is resolute and focused solely on revenge.

500–16 In one final extraordinary act in an extraordinary scene, Othello kneels and swears an oath to seek his revenge as if he were a chivalrous lover pledging himself to a quest. This may even exceed Iago's own expectation of what he could make Othello do. A thought occurs to Iago, he can use this moment to commit Othello once and for all. Seeing that Othello is about to get up, Iago stops him, and kneels himself. Iago solemnly offers his own service, asking the audience to serve as witness to his loyalty. Iago deliberately goes a little further than Othello. Othello only promises never to let his rage slip back into love until he has revenge. Iago knows that this must mean bloodshed.

They are no longer General and Ancient, master and servant, but confederates in a secret murder plot.

517–end Standing again, Othello seems almost like his old self when he orders Iago to kill Cassio. Iago does not flinch from the order, but he reminds Othello that Cassio is a friend. Othello is momentarily provoked into another fit of anger when Iago begs Othello to let Desdemona live (does he mean it?). But Othello quickly recovers himself, and readies himself to kill her. Iago finally achieves the rank of Lieutenant, and perhaps Iago is sincere when he accepts it. This is what he has wanted since the start of the play. The audience will expect another triumphant soliloquy from Iago to close off the scene, but instead Iago follows Othello out. Does he acknowledge the audience as he does so? Does he need the audience anymore?

Act III, scene iv

1–22 The scene begins with a brief comic banter between Desdemona and a clown. These lines are usually cut from the performance as they add little to the story. The clown does not bring in Cassio as promised (Iago does) and the exchange between him and Desdemona seems disconnected from the following lines.

23–33 Desdemona is worried about losing her handkerchief and sounds frustrated, as if she has been looking for it already. Crucially, Emilia lies to her at l.24. Desdemona still trusts Othello – but she may be a little concerned when Emilia says that she sees him approaching.

34–9 Othello can barely contain himself anymore, it is an effort to even be civil to Desdemona and when he looks at her – *if* he looks at her – he will see only his own despair and anger.

Desdemona has judged this the moment to push hard on Cassio's case, Othello has decided to test her on the handkerchief. The scene begins with both of them trying to find their way in to what they want to say, and ends with them shouting at each other, Othello demanding to know where the handkerchief is, Desdemona desperately trying (and failing) to change the conversation to talk about Cassio. Their asides fragment the dialogue and reveal the distance between them.

40–52 Othello takes Desdemona's hand. His actions might be those of a lover, but they are laced with an unspoken sense of threat. He holds Desdemona's hand for longer than he should, making this affectionate gesture awkward and uncomfortable. Why is he fascinated with her hand? There's something mad about Othello's behaviour. The audience knows what he is imagining as he strokes her hand.

Desdemona is uneasy. She tries to find some tenderness in Othello's behaviour, but withdraws her hand at l.52, refusing to speak any further about it.

52–61 Desdemona turns instead (unfortunately) to Cassio. Othello reacts physically to the sound of his Lieutenant's name. Whether faked or not, he uses this response as a pretext to force Desdemona to bring out her handkerchief and stop talking about Cassio.

Desdemona does not have the handkerchief. The next lines (ll.56–61) are short and fragmented. Othello is still testing Desdemona (as she begins to realise). Othello's paranoia deepens. He sees more evidence of fault in Desdemona's answers.

62–95 Othello makes a nasty and unsubtle attempt to put Desdemona in her place. His story is a scarcely believable tale of a strawberry handkerchief transformed into an exotic family heirloom made by a prophetess out of sacred silk and died with the mummified blood of maidens. Desdemona is stupefied by this story. Her brief interjections can signify either her incredulity, or her deepening horror, or both. Othello is not now speaking as he did in Act I when recalling the stories he had wooed Desdemona with. This is a threatening, mad speech, which inches teasingly to the moment at l.87 when Othello finally lets out his rage with a barely comprehensible question which he presses again and again on Desdemona, who is stunned by Othello's behaviour and melts, insisting that she has lost the handkerchief.

96–108 Desdemona recovers herself, and tries once more to turn the conversation back to Cassio. This is just a trick, this nonsense about a handkerchief, you are just avoiding the subject. Othello will not be talked to – he demands the handkerchief again. And now, bizarrely, Desdemona starts to talk about Cassio anyway. Desdemona and Othello are talking at cross-purposes so much in this exchange that they are virtually in different scenes. They do not talk to each other, just *at* each other. Desdemona carries on, almost nagging, ignoring Othello, who finally throws his hands up and walks away swearing.

109–16 Emilia is neither surprised nor concerned by Othello's behaviour. This is typical of men, she sniffs. Desdemona does not know what to make of Othello at all. She does not know whether to be upset, offended, worried or just puzzled. Why all this concern over a handkerchief?

Emilia's disenchmantment with her own marriage breaks through in a compelling image of marriage as a meal, in which the wife is digested and then belched out. She might be talking to herself, reflecting on her own disappointment with Iago. She might also be trying to enlist Desdemona as a companion with similar marital problems. Iago, the subject of Emilia's derision, chooses this moment to enter, and Emilia notices him wearily. She says nothing to him for more than 20 lines. Do they even acknowledge each other?

117–19 Iago is dragging a reluctant Cassio with him. Iago is in full flow, he is trying to persuade Cassio to appeal to Desdemona again. He gestures towards her, and Cassio (perhaps nervously) approaches.

120–33 Desdemona seems genuinely glad to see Cassio, but she has little good news for him. Cassio remains anxious, he does not want things to go on any longer, he is desperate to know one way or the other whether Othello will forgive him.

134–43 Desdemona has little comfort and admits for the first time that Othello will not listen to her, that he is not himself. She offers kind reassurance that she will continue to importune Othello, but Cassio must be patient. Cassio does not react and says nothing more to Desdemona until she leaves. There is nothing more that he can say.

144–52 Desdemona has attracted Iago's interest. Iago cannot wait to see Othello's 'strange' behaviour for himself and so he makes an awkward excuse to leave, hardly waiting for Desdemona's blessing. Iago risks letting his excitement betray him. He asks if Othello is angry four times. He passes this off as an expression of his concern, but the truth is that Iago is delighted that Othello's madness continues even when Iago is not there to drive him on.

153–81 Desdemona is still trying to understand Othello's words and actions. She thinks through several possibilities: maybe it is work that is making him unlike himself, he's just taking it out on me, I should not think bad of him for this. Emilia's responses do not reassure her. She says I hope you're right, I hope it is not jealousy. Emilia's contribution to the discussion echoes Iago's in the previous scene, as does her cynical, disenchanted attitude towards men and marriage. Worried now, Desdemona decides that, like Iago, she will look for Othello, and leaves Cassio to himself.

182–end Bianca is an unexpected addition to the play. A no-nonsense and feisty working girl, Bianca should be explosive. Cassio starts to apologise, but only because he wants Bianca to copy the pattern on the handkerchief. Bianca is insulted and assumes (as Othello also does later) that the handkerchief is a love token from another mistress. Cassio then accuses *her* of jealousy and refuses to be drawn on who the handkerchief belongs to. It will not help Cassio's suit to Othello to be found in public with this woman: he must get rid of her.

Act IV

Act IV, scene i

1–20 Othello now belongs entirely to Iago, who twists Othello's deranged mind still further. We find them in the middle of talking,

Iago pulling again at Othello's paranoia and doubts. A kiss? Naked in bed? And the handkerchief? Iago is *telling* Othello what to think. Othello has no will of his own in these lines, no choice but to believe everything Iago says. The handkerchief affects Othello more than anything else. He is preoccupied with it, perhaps because the handkerchief is the only certain thing he can latch on to.

21–4   Othello briefly tries to put it all out of his mind, to forget everything, but as soon as he pushes his thoughts away they fly back at him: he had *my* handkerchief.

25–41   Iago pushes Othello even further. He has heard Cassio say something . . . then Iago skirts round what is said. Othello must hear Cassio's words even though he already *knows* what Iago is going to say. He probes and pushes Iago, who finally says what he has been implying since this all started in Act III. The moment has come for Iago to risk everything and say, bluntly, that Desdemona is unfaithful. If he had said this in Act III, Othello would not have believed him. Now, Othello would be angry if he said anything but this. Just in case (and to maintain the facade of an honest man struggling with hard truths) Iago dresses his comments in evasions and qualifications. In fact, Iago never explicitly says that Cassio slept with Desdemona, but he says enough to drive Othello into a bitter, bewildered rage.

42–50   Othello's next words tumble out, he is incoherent, incandescent, his monster is released – and he falls into a fit, giving Iago a momentary chance to marvel at his own work. Othello's fall is Iago's masterpiece. But Iago does not give himself too long to congratulate himself, as there is still work to be done.

51–65   Cassio comes on to the stage to find Othello collapsed and Iago standing by him. Iago's lines give us some directions for Othello's behaviour: he should be inert, almost in a coma. Cassio either tries to help Othello or at least urges Iago to, but Iago holds him back. Iago reassures him that Othello has had fits like this before and just needs to be left alone. Iago is probably telling the truth, since he is not concerned about Othello's health and he should be, for his plans cannot be completed if Othello dies now. Othello starts to wake up, so Iago hurries Cassio off the stage (much as he had done Roderigo in earlier scenes) before turning back to Othello.

66–83   Othello comes to and may be clutching his head, as Iago asks him if he has hurt it. Othello takes this as an insulting reference to a cuckold's horns but Iago insists that he is not making fun of him. Othello's manner is less forceful, the fit has taken the immediate violence of his anger away and he is instead brooding and withdrawn as he slowly recovers consciousness. Othello has not forgotten what made him faint, so he asks Iago, has Cassio admitted the affair? Iago's answer is as evasive as ever, and he concludes with an elliptical couplet that uses the same words in different places in a deliberate attempt to baffle Othello, who must admit that Iago is 'wise'.

84–104   Othello can stand at any point after first coming to, but he must be standing by l.84. Othello may show another flash of anger when Iago mentions that Cassio had come by, but Othello is quiet for the rest of these lines. He is exhausted by anger, and ready to let Iago tell him what to do and where to go. Iago explains his plan, and vividly describes what Othello should do: study Cassio's face and gestures, look for any and every sign of guilt. Now is not the time for anger, but for patience. Othello submits, he has no choice to because he has lost all capacity for rational thought. His temper flares briefly before he retreats to a hiding place.

105–11   Othello hides, but not from the audience: wherever he is onstage, the audience must be able to see and hear him. The stage picture is now very complex. The audience watches Othello watching Iago and Cassio. They also see Iago deliberately manipulating Cassio, knowing that some of what he says will be for Othello's benefit. Iago will have to find ways to conceal some aspects of their conversation so that Othello never realises that they are talking about Bianca instead of Desdemona. To add to this complexity, Iago starts by stepping out of the frame of the action (perhaps literally) to tell the audience what he plans to do. The audience also learns a little more about Bianca.

112–57   Cassio enters at l.112, and for the next three lines Iago speaks to the audience with Cassio approaching, Othello watching. Iago will modulate his voice carefully so that l.118, when he mentions

Desdemona, will be heard clearly by Othello, but the following two lines (about Bianca) will not. Iago can either lower his voice (as some editions suggest) or simply walk Cassio about the stage, or take him aside to whisper conspiratorially.

Cassio is gloomy when he enters, but Iago's jokes about Bianca set him off laughing. As far as Cassio is concerned, Iago is just trying to cheer him up. Othello watches and comments on the action. Iago will be acutely aware of Othello's gaze for the whole exchange and will be playing up to it. Cassio rallies when he talks about Bianca and then, strangely (though not so strange to Othello who already believes that Cassio has a habit of treating Iago as if were Desdemona) Cassio starts to pretend to be Bianca and embraces Iago (what does Iago make of this sudden familiarity?). All this Othello completely misinterprets. Iago's plan has worked so far, but when Bianca enters, the plan is jeopardised.

158–72 Everything could go wrong now, but fortunately for Iago, Bianca comes in waving Desdemona's handkerchief and shouting at Cassio for giving her some other woman's love token. Although Bianca is obviously the woman that Cassio has been talking to Iago about, Othello is too struck by the sight of the handkerchief to realise this. He is hypnotised by the handkerchief, which Bianca petulantly thrusts into Cassio's hands. She refuses to listen to Cassio's half-hearted attempt to calm her down.

173–80 Iago insists that Cassio go after Bianca, even though Cassio is more worried about how she could ruin his reputation than he is about upsetting her. He still intends to visit her at the brothel, and Iago, it appears, will meet him there.

Iago is anxious to get rid of Cassio now. He has achieved everything he wanted to and to talk any further with Othello watching is too risky. When he says 'say no more' (l.180) he means it.

181–91 All doubt is gone. Othello comes out of the shadows full of murderous certainty. There is no need now for Iago to pretend to defend Cassio, he can slander and plot murder freely with Othello, who defers to him completely.

Iago is still concerned that Othello might not be fully committed, so he makes him reflect on what Cassio has just done and said. When he talks about Cassio, Othello grows angry. However, when he talks about Desdemona, Othello finds himself drawn back to reflecting on her virtues. Othello wavers between love and hate, and each time Iago insists that Othello stay focused on Desdemona's faults.

192–222 Othello announces that he will kill Desdemona. Othello now becomes urgent. The murder must take place tonight, and he has decided to use poison. Delighted, Iago quickly revises Othello's plan. He is no longer restraining Othello or pretending that there might be some other way to deal with Desdemona. That Iago has gone – *this* Iago pushes Othello to go even further. Don't just poison her, *strangle* her, he says, and in the same bed she slept with Cassio in. Othello is perversely enjoying talking about revenge. He is now so focused on Desdemona that he has forgotten about Cassio, whom Iago promises to take care of. All the anger Othello earlier directed at Cassio is now firmly pointed at Desdemona.

223–31 Events are now ready to move to their conclusion. The sound of a trumpet heralds Lodovico's arrival from Venice and he enters with Desdemona, who will be playing hostess. This is a sudden and unexpected development which may throw both Othello and Iago momentarily. They have been locked in their paranoid fantasies, but now the stage opens up to a wider social world in which they have to play their part. Lodovico has a letter which Othello reads privately with evident concern.

232–50 As Othello buries himself in the letter, Lodovico asks after Cassio. This prompts Desdemona to briefly talk about the rift that has opened up between Cassio and Othello. Othello suddenly interrupts with a line that Desdemona takes to be a comment on the way she has described the situation. Perhaps she is right, but Othello's next line is a quote from the letter. Lodovico assures her that Othello is just reacting to the news from Venice.

At l.246 there is a deliberate ambiguity about whether Othello is reacting to the letter, or to Desdemona's talk of the 'love' she has for Cassio. Either are legitimate readings. Lodovico assumes Othello is angry about instructions in the letter, but Desdemona may not be so sure.

251–65 Lodovico explains that the letter recalls Othello and puts Cassio in charge of Cyprus. This evidently pleases Desdemona, and her response to this news infuriates Othello, who uses her own words back at her. Desdemona tries to be patient and tender with Othello (l.255), but he curses and strikes her. Desdemona retreats, crying. Lodovico is astonished and tries to get Othello to apologise, but Othello continues to rant.

266–82 Desdemona collects herself enough to try and leave the stage. Lodovico, still stunned, begs Othello to call her back. Othello mocks him by shouting after Desdemona. What do you want me to do with her, he snarls to Lodovico? With no answer, Othello rails at Desdemona's tears and mocks her obedience, and then orders her to leave. Othello's behaviour is painful and embarrassing to watch. Othello has lost all sense of the line between public and private, and all sense of himself.

Lodovico must be astonished. Othello acts like a split subject. He talks to Lodovico about arrangements for his return to Venice, and then in the same breath shouts again at Desdemona, who does not know what to do or how to react. Othello is trying to show that he is only angry with Desdemona. He has not lost his mind and can conduct his duties and still take his revenge.

283–86 Othello assents to the letter's orders and invites Lodovico to dinner. He is not polite for long and leaves the stage again cursing.

286–end Lodovico looks after Othello utterly amazed at what he has seen. Can this be the same Othello? Iago takes the opportunity to spin a little more mischief, saying that there is more that could be said, but he must be silent. Lodovico is shaken, and Iago prepares him for worse to come.

Act IV, scene ii

This scene takes place just before the dinner that is held for the Venetians. All characters will be dressed ready for this occasion.

1–11 Othello is questioning Emilia about Desdemona's behaviour. His questions are abrupt, and none of Emilia's answers satisfy him.

The scene starts with Othello in the middle of his interrogation. We do not know how long he has been hounding Emilia, or how blunt he has been with her. Othello is clearly suspicious about Desdemona and Cassio, and Emilia is quick to assure him of Desdemona's honesty.

The questions are quick and Othello puts them aggressively. In l.3 he does not so much ask a question as provide an answer and insist that Emilia agrees to it. Emilia refuses: yes, of course she has seen Desdemona and Cassio together, but there was nothing between them and she heard every word that they said. Othello seizes on this obvious weakness: surely she could not have heard *everything* said, they must have whispered *something* between them. When Emilia insists that they did not, Othello tries another tack. Perhaps they sent Emilia away? He is astonished by Emilia's answers and pushes again and again, but Emilia is resolute.

12 Othello is puzzled. He does not understand how Emilia could miss evidence of Desdemona's affair. Intriguingly, Othello does not suspect that Emilia is lying. The thought that Emilia might be protecting her mistress does not even occur to him. Madness has overtaken Othello. Desdemona's adultery is now so self-evident to him that he can hardly believe that it is not obvious to everybody. Emilia's ignorance neither reassures him, nor does it increase his paranoia. Instead, he treats her story as a paradox. How could it be possible for Emilia not to see what must self-evidently be true?

13–20 Tired of answering questions, Emilia makes as clear a statement as she can about Desdemona. Othello may not even be listening, so wrapped up is he in his own thoughts and fantasies. Yet these are important lines, this is the closest to the truth that Othello has come in the play. No one has yet explicitly asserted Desdemona's innocence, and Emilia here sets herself up for the role she will eventually play in Act V. She can say all these lines with certainty, but the audience will be alive to the irony that the serpent she talks of is her own husband, and that she has played a key part in his plan.

21 Othello sends her away to fetch Desdemona. He shows no signs of having even listened to Emilia. She might as well have been talking to the air. By including this speech, Shakespeare makes it harder for Othello to be absolved of responsibility for his own actions. Yes, he is led on by Iago, but here Emilia tells him the truth. Desdemona is innocent, she insists, and anybody that says otherwise is a 'wretch'. That Othello hears this, but does not listen, makes him more culpable.

22–25 With Emilia gone, Othello reflects on what her strange answers might mean. There are two ways to read the following lines, and Othello's thinking is now so hard to penetrate, so far from reason, that either can be played. He either suspects that Emilia is lying to him, or he concludes that she is stupid and that this is just part of (and further evidence of) Desdemona's dishonesty.

Everything turns on who the 'subtle whore' is in l.23. Othello starts by acknowledging that Emilia has said all the right things to make Desdemona's behaviour seem above reproach. However, even a 'simple bawd' could answer his questions like this. He either means that Emilia has been easily fooled, or that any woman could try and fool him. Can Emilia be both the 'simple bawd' and the 'subtle whore' that Othello now ruminates on, who locks her secrets away, and yet has the hypocrisy to pray? Editors are divided over whether the 'whore' is Emilia or Desdemona. For me, there are more interesting possibilities in reading it as a reference to Desdemona, as it is she with whom Othello is obsessed. Both readings are available to the actor, and the lines might work best if their ambiguity is preserved for the audience. Othello's mind is now beyond being read rationally.

Othello's last words are a rhetorical flourish that return us to his obsession with 'ocular proof'. He has seen her praying, which in his eyes is enough to condemn her. He says this mad thought as if he is trying to convince someone, but who could that be: the audience, or himself?

26–30 Desdemona enters accompanied by Emilia. We now see Othello at his most unguarded. In his own mind, he may even feel he his is being completely open now, but Desdemona is simply frightened by his erratic temper.

Ll.26–29 are written as half-lines, with Othello completing Desdemona's verse lines, then Desdemona completing Othello's. Shakespeare sometimes uses this device to hint at an erotic connection between two characters, but here the effect is to twist this love story into something darker and, as Desdemona puts it, 'horrible'. The lines suggest the stage action. Desdemona must be nervous about approaching Othello, who tells her to 'come hither' (using the word 'pray' lightly, but perhaps with a hint of irony given what Othello has just been saying about prayer). Neither Desdemona nor Othello rush to greet each other as they would have done earlier in the play: this alone is enough to signal how much trouble they are in.

There is something taunting about Othello's commands, especially when he demands to see her eyes (l.29). He may hold her face. Desdemona certainly has cause to recoil, as she calls Othello's actions a 'horrible' fancy (l.30). What is horrible about this? A loving husband might ask to look into his wife's eyes, but Othello does not do so lovingly. This is an action worth experimenting with. The text leaves it to the actors to decide how to play the action, and their decisions will deepen our understanding of the characters and their relationship. Does Othello hold her face, stare into her eyes and maintain his stare too long? Does Desdemona try to resist, is she pulled back, does she escape? When does she say l.30: when Othello is still looking into her eyes, or afterwards? Does he walk away from her, or is he still staring when he says his next lines to Emilia? How does Emilia respond to this awkward, unpleasant moment? What is Othello looking for when he stares into Desdemona's eyes, what does he find and what does he think he finds? There are no answers to these questions and the actors should strive to preserve this ambiguity and instil in what was once a romantic gesture a real sense of menace.

31–4   Othello now wants rid of Emilia and puts her in her place, treating her like a servant. He speaks as if he and Desdemona want privacy to make love but, as we soon learn, he says this with a 'fury' in his voice. They are 'procreants' (a functional word for 'lovers') and need to be left alone. He acts as if they are still secret lovers, but surely neither Desdemona nor Emilia believe this. This is a moment of suspense for the audience as well: Othello is alone with Desdemona, will he kill her now?

35–52   Shakespeare has Desdemona kneel for these lines, but the actors are free to decide when and how she kneels, and when she rises again. With a very simple edit or cut in l.35, Desdemona does not have to kneel at all. Much will depend on how the rest of this passage is played. The scene can be fast-paced, full of anger and imminent threat, but it can just as easily be drawn out and painful to watch. Othello is reaching an emotional pitch and he is crying (as Desdemona's words tell us) by l.46.

Desdemona begins admitting she is baffled and worried by Othello's words. She does not know what he means, but she knows he is upset. Desdemona kneels to placate Othello.

Othello is so deep into his own fears and fantasies that he does not respond to anything that Desdemona says. Instead, he attacks her with questions which reveal the depths of his own self-doubts. L.37 is a despairing, unanswerable question, and Desdemona's response just makes him incredulous. Swear it, he says, not because he wants reassurance, but because with each lie (as he sees it), Desdemona becomes more and more the devil woman he is now utterly convinced she must be. She is not only an adulterer, but a blasphemer too. There is nothing that Desdemona can do or say to pull Othello back. He is completely lost, and anything he hears or sees will reinforce his madness.

If Desdemona starts in a submissive, conciliatory way, she does not remain like this, and decides to answer back. Desdemona can sometimes be played as a weak character, but here she shows her strength. Othello cries, not Desdemona. She answers honestly and with conviction, she swears that she is 'true and loyal' and when Othello calls her 'false' she retorts with questions of her own (l.45). These are questions that Othello cannot answer, perhaps because he cannot bear to say the words, either to her or perhaps even to himself. Instead, overcome with tears, he tells her to go (l.46). He calls her Desdemon and perhaps emphasises the 'demon' in her name.

Desdemona asks more questions, but now she shows her concern for Othello, who is clearly distraught. She even offers to disown her father.

53–70 Othello ignores Desdemona. This long speech is not spoken to her, or to the audience, or even to himself. He addresses Heaven, Patience and Time, looking for something to direct his anger against. He is not yet ready or able to drive it at Desdemona: when he does, he will kill her.

There are two parts to the speech. Ll.53–58 echo the stories with which Othello first seduced Desdemona as he imagines what torments he could endure. With l.60, he reveals his sense of humiliation, as if Time itself is pointing at him, and Othello is a figure outside of Time. In the Quarto text, Othello says 'Oh, oh' at this point, as if groaning at the thought of his own ruin. The next part seems to contradict what he has just said. I could bear even that fate, he says, and then his thoughts and words meander. The next lines will be obscure to most audiences, and they are meant to be. Othello is beyond rational thought. L.60's 'there' may be directed at Desdemona – that is where he has put his soul, his fate, that is where Patience should look, it is Desdemona who is 'grim as hell'. Desdemona is the fountain which has either dried up or become a cistern for 'foul toads'.

71–77 How does Desdemona react? Before, she was conciliatory, caring. Now she defends herself. Between these two moments, Desdemona has come to realise that she is in danger, that she needs to be more concerned about herself and her own reputation than about Othello. Her lines in this passage are increasingly forthright: she starts at l.71 with a line which may be said angrily, even though the words are deferential. Othello's next lines are very insulting, and Desdemona's response is more defensive. She again tries to turn the tables on Othello, she asks him a question, which he again refuses to answer. However, Desdemona is still assuming that Othello has a reason for being angry with her. If she has committed a sin, she is ignorant of it.

78–87 If Othello was being reasonable, he would seize on Desdemona's claim that she does not know what sin she is guilty of, but instead he seizes on one word: 'committed'. He does not answer Desdemona's question, he just rages at it, and repeats it leaving out entirely the reference to 'ignorant sin'. He calls her a whore, a common prostitute, he acts as if her actions were so foul that not only can he not say what they are, but Heaven, the Earth and the Moon itself do not want to hear it said. This is an absurd argument, Othello has fallen into a ridiculous state of mind, and Desdemona is appalled at his words. For the first time, she realises that she has done nothing knowingly or unknowingly to deserve this.

88–103 Desdemona defends herself against Othello's insults and insists that she is not a 'strumpet'. Othello is incredulous, and he asks essentially the same question three times. He does not once believe Desdemona's answers; instead he mocks them with more questions.

At l.96, Desdemona seems to give in. She has been standing up for herself, but she is no match for Othello's needling interrogation. Othello treats her like an upstart. If she is innocent, he says witheringly, he apologises, he mistook her for Desdemona.

Emilia enters at some point during these lines (see Chapter 1 for a discussion of the implications of *when* Emilia enters). Othello is done. He treats Emilia like a money-grabbing servant, denigrating her by tossing her a coin and telling her to keep their secret. Othello acts as if he and Desdemona are still having an illicit affair. Perhaps Emilia did once help the lovers to meet in secret, standing watch as they made love. If so, Othello appears to mock their courtship by replaying it like this. Othello exits the stage full of spiteful anger.

104–17   Emilia tries and fails to get sense out of Desdemona. Emilia has heard Othello call Desdemona a whore, and her first question is a leading one. Emilia wants Desdemona to tell her what happened, but she refuses to. Like Othello, Desdemona's thoughts are now beyond being spoken.

Desdemona is in shock. She does not know how to react, she cannot cry, and nothing that she has said to Othello explains his actions. Her lines in this passage reflect her distracted mind. Desdemona says little to Emilia. In fact, in her own way, Desdemona is beginning to sound a little like Othello. Her thoughts are wandering and fragmented, she gives evasive answers to direct questions almost as if she does not hear them, she asks leading questions and then ignores their answers, and she gives instructions to Emilia as if she were a servant rather than her closest companion. Desdemona is neither as angry nor as mad as Othello, but now she seems to be copying him. She even wants to see Iago.

117   Emilia does not push too hard and withdraws to get Iago. She notices the 'change', which can either be a reference to Desdemona's character, to the marriage, or to the way Desdemona treats Emilia.

118–20   Desdemona now has a short speech to herself. This is her only soliloquy in the play, but it tells us very little. With Emilia gone, Desdemona feels more able to reveal her own anger at being damned for nothing. L.118 could be played as if Desdemona is accepting Othello's view of her, but the next lines suggest that she does not, in which case it might be more effective to speak the lines sarcastically. In the next couplet, Desdemona describes Othello and his action with contempt, something she does not do elsewhere. Only when alone does she mock his 'small'st opinion' (this could also be read as a comment on his sexual abilities).

121–27 The following section returns to the three-way banter of 2.1, when Iago teased Desdemona and Emilia with his bawdy jokes. This time the tone is much darker. The scene is overshadowed by tragic irony, since Desdemona and Emilia both turn to Iago for help. Does Emilia suspect her husband at all? When she speculates about the 'villainous knave' who has abused the Moor, is she looking at Iago for a reaction, or is Iago's deception so complete that he can see Desdemona this distraught, listen to his own wife say these things, and not be at all moved?

Desdemona is still behaving a bit like Othello, albeit without the anger. Iago's question (l.122) gets no clearer answer out of Desdemona than Emilia did. Desdemona gives a distracted answer, and despairs that she has not been treated gently like a child should be. Iago tries again (l.127) and Emilia answers for her. Clearly Emilia knows exactly what is going on because she heard Othello before. Iago of course also knows (or can guess) what has happened. Both of their questions are redundant.

128–31 Iago will be pleased to hear Emilia say these lines. Things are going to plan, and he may acknowledge his satisfaction to the audience. With Emilia putting the situation bluntly, Desdemona asks Iago directly if she is 'that name', still unable to say the word 'whore' herself.

132–38 Iago draws out the following exchange for longer than necessary. Emilia is too indignant to let this carry on, and says plainly that Othello called her a whore. Iago does not answer Emilia but turns back to Desdemona with an ambiguous question, which is superficially sympathetic but could be read in a more accusatory way. Desdemona gives in to her emotions and starts crying, for Iago now tells her to stop weeping.

139–49 Desdemona melts into tears, and Iago is uncharacteristically quiet, his part reduced to brief interjections more typical of a supernumerary than a main part, a Montano rather than an Iago. What does Iago do in these next lines? Does he comfort Desdemona, or does he stand back awkwardly, unable to deal with Desdemona like this?

Whatever he does, Emilia takes advantage of the silence to speak her mind. Apart from a few short comments from Iago and Desdemona, Emilia has the stage for the next 20 lines, and she uses her time to speculate wildly about the man who has put Othello up to this.

150–51 Iago and Desdemona's responses are fascinatingly different and tell us much about their characters. Iago is quick to deny that there could be any such person (he is of course denying himself) at l.150, and at l.151 Desdemona prays for forgiveness (though maybe not sincerely) for whoever has led Othello on.

152–65 Emilia will not hear of any pardon, and carries on lambasting the 'notorious knave'. The speech is evidently making Iago uncomfortable. Emilia is coming too close to the truth. Her voice might be getting louder, for Iago first tells her to be quiet, then tells her (in effect) to shut up, insulting her at the same time. The attention must be on Desdemona, not on him.

166–83 The scene's focus now switches back to Desdemona. Emilia obeys Iago and says nothing more for the rest of the scene, though she may resent him for using his authority so insultingly. Desdemona seems not to notice their tiff, but has collected herself enough to speak at some length about her fears. Like Othello, she places her trust in Iago and even echoes Othello by now kneeling in front of Iago to implore him to help her. Shakespeare gives no direction for Desdemona to stand again, but she must do so before she leaves the stage.

Desdemona states her innocence as clearly and unambiguously as she can. She says to Iago what she was either unable or not ready to say to Othello earlier in the scene.

Desdemona structures her first sentence as if it were a legal statement. She speaks in the language of a proclamation or a judicial sentence. There is, perhaps, an echo of traditional marriage vows in her words, as every qualification and exception is anticipated in one phrase. Desdemona finally says the word 'whore', but even as she speaks it she loathes herself for saying it. The word will be a hard one for her to say, and she seems to snatch it back when she 'abhors' it.

184–89 Iago's response is to try and play down the significance of the moment. Othello has had a bad day at work, he tells Desdemona, she is crying over nothing. Iago wants now to be rid of Desdemona and Emilia. He has little patience with their emotions, and both have come too near to the truth for comfort. Desdemona tries to carry on speaking, but he quickly interrupts her and uses the sound of trumpets as an excuse to get both women off the stage.

Desdemona's scene should have lasted longer, there is much more to say, and Iago has not answered Desdemona's plea to 'go to' Othello.

The trumpets are announcing the start of the dinner being held for the Venetian visitors, and Iago sends Desdemona and Emilia in to the dinner. This means that they will have to ready themselves for an important audience, Desdemona in particular will have to hide her emotions to play hostess. Moreover, she will have to face Othello again.

190–236 Roderigo now enters. The text does not tell us how or why, but Iago catches him. This is the last time that Roderigo and Iago talk at length, and their exchange is little more than a recap of the earlier scenes, as if Shakespeare is giving the audiences a final opportunity to watch Iago gull the hapless Roderigo. The scene unfolds in an almost identical way to their first scene together in 1.1. Roderigo is upset that none of the jewels he has given Iago to woo Desdemona with have made her any better disposed to him. Iago's plan has failed. Of course, Iago has pocketed all the jewels. There is opportunity here for comedy as the audience will immediately guess what has really happened. The thought never occurs to Roderigo though, but he is angry that Iago's plans have come to nothing; he is now broke as well as lovelorn.

Compared to Othello, Roderigo is an easy character to manipulate. Iago enjoys working on him, he could probably get Roderigo to do anything, including murder. Iago lets Roderigo rant for a while, interjecting only occasionally. If Iago is concerned that Roderigo might act on his promise to demand the jewels back from Desdemona he does not show it. Instead, he works to rebuild Roderigo's confidence: he takes Roderigo's hand and protests that he has been working hard on his suit. To show how serious he is, Iago even promises, as sincerely as he can, that Roderigo will have Desdemona by the next night. Roderigo is a little taken aback by this – but he is hooked. What is Iago's plan?

237–end Iago now explains that Othello is soon to leave Cyprus with Desdemona and to stop this happening, Roderigo needs to kill Cassio. Roderigo is not immediately convinced by this as a plan, but allows Iago to explain it.

This is not one of Iago's better ruses and he has to improvise to keep Roderigo hooked. Roderigo is happy when he thinks Othello and Desdemona are heading back to Venice. He has had enough of Cyprus. To put Roderigo off, Iago tells him that Othello has been posted to Mauritania. When Iago casually talks about 'removing' Cassio, Roderigo asks him what he means. Iago is now as blunt as he ever is, and may even fail to hide his enthusiasm at the thought of bludgeoning his rival Cassio. This is risky indeed – until now Roderigo has done what he has been told, but he has never killed anyone. He is clearly stunned, as Iago tells him to 'stand not amazed' (l.257) and by the scene's end Roderigo has still not agreed to the plan. He has not said no either. Iago makes haste, hoping that if he acts with haste and urgency, Roderigo will not have time to think too much.

Act IV, scene iii

A production looking for substantial cuts could remove this scene and the exchange between Iago and Roderigo which closes 4.2 and move straight on to 5.1. However, this would cut one of the best written and most affecting scenes in the play. The scene is both tender and terrible. It brilliantly contrasts the mundane domestic activity of getting ready for bed with the sense of menace which both Desdemona and Emilia feel. What is not said is much more important than what is said. Emilia chats away about men and marriage as she gets Desdemona ready for bed. Desdemona listens and sings to herself, but the magnitude of her situation cannot be escaped.

1–12 These lines establish the time and place. The dinner party is over and Othello walks out with Lodovico, perhaps escorting him to his lodgings. Desdemona and Emilia are with them. The party must have been an ordeal for everyone, especially Desdemona, who would have had to put on a public face even though Othello would probably have ignored her for most of the evening. The strain may be showing now that they are away from their guests.

The tone is only superficially convivial. Lodovico tries to politely reject Othello's offer. He is still concerned about Othello's attitude towards Desdemona, and is either keen to avoid being alone with him, or he does not want to give Othello an excuse to ignore Desdemona. The lines also suggest that Othello is keeping his distance from Desdemona. Only at the end does he suddenly turn to Desdemona, giving her a curt order almost as an afterthought.

This is the last time that Othello and Desdemona are seen in public together so there is an opportunity for the cast to create visual rhymes with their first appearance in 1.3. Lodovico is leaving on one side of the stage, Emilia is waiting for Desdemona on the other. Emilia does not hear what Othello says to Desdemona (as we learn in the next lines) and there is no reason that Lodovico should hear either. Othello could make a show of affection for the benefit of the guests, holding Desdemona's hand one last time.

13–17 Emilia at least seems to think Othello is behaving better, but Desdemona quickly disabuses her and tells her that Othello does not want her to stay. He will return soon (the word 'incontinent' can be changed to 'immediately' to clarify the meaning of l.14 for modern audiences).

The meaning of l.17 changes depending on which word is stressed. Is Emilia worried about being dismissed, or is she affronted that Othello (and Desdemona) are treating her like a common servant?

18–22 Desdemona could sympathise with Emilia, but instead she reiterates Othello's instruction. Desdemona is determined to stay loyal to her husband. She asks Emilia to help her into her night things and then leave. Emilia is clearly upset and says she wishes Desdemona had never seen Othello. This is a bold thing to say, and although Desdemona disagrees with her, she does not take offence as she might have done if Emilia had said such a thing in Act II.

22–29   As Desdemona begins to get ready for bed, she tells Emilia
that she loves Othello even when he is angry. However, Desdemona
may not be fully convinced herself as she digresses to ask Emilia to
'unpin' her (either loosening her hair or her dress). Is she coming
apart in other ways as well? Desdemona seeks refuge in romantic
thoughts and domestic business, but darker thoughts keep breaking
through. When Emilia says that she has put some sheets on the bed,
Desdemona morbidly asks to be buried in them. Emilia tells her off.

30–39   Desdemona continues to talk in a slightly distracted way.
Her thoughts are being inevitably drawn towards tragic stories even
though she avoids talking about herself and her problems. Her mind
is full of a song about unrequited love and mortal despair that
she learnt from her mother's maid. Emilia will be attending her as
she speaks, getting her ready for bed. At l.37, Desdemona suddenly
tells Emilia to hurry up. Emilia asks if Desdemona wants her night-
gown, but Desdemona asks her to just finish helping her to undress.
Desdemona is anxious to get ready because she expects Othello to
return soon.

40–44   Desdemona and Emilia briefly distract themselves with
small talk about Lodovico. This is a bit of inconsequential gossip
which some productions cut. However, these lines show Desdemona
and Emilia trying to behave normally despite the impending threat.

45–52   Desdemona cannot help herself from falling into the song
that is haunting her. The melody and full lyrics of the song are
included in some editions of the play. As she sings, Emilia will still
be helping her to get ready for bed. The song begins to break apart
(as perhaps does Desdemona) when she sings about 'salt tears'.

53–59   Desdemona stops singing briefly to give Emilia an instruction, she starts again, then stops to tell Emilia to hurry up. She sang
the song to calm herself, but she cannot forget that Othello is coming
soon. Desdemona starts to sing again but stumbles when she sings a
line that is not in the song. L.57 echoes the words Desdemona said
to Emilia at ll.22–24. She has become the subject of her song. The
thought causes Desdemona to stop, she does not know why she sang
that line. Suddenly, she starts, thinking someone is knocking at the

door. Is it Othello? Emilia reassures her that there is no one at the door, she can just hear the wind. From the audience's point of view, it may work best if there is no noise for Desdemona to hear. She is so anxious that she is jumping at shadows.

60–66 Desdemona resumes her song, but she does not last long. She stops, saying her eyes are itching. She is trying hard to control herself, she does not want to give in to despair and fear. Curiously, she asks if itchy eyes are a symptom of imminent tears. Emilia has no answer to give her.

66–78 The last lines of the song (ll.60–62) had been about infidelity. The thought stays in Desdemona's mind and she now raises it with Emilia. She is curious about women who have affairs. To even talk about this is, for Desdemona, touching on a taboo subject. Emilia avoids answering Desdemona at l.70, which provokes Desdemona to ask if *Emilia* would sleep with another man. Emilia teases her in reply, and when Desdemona insists that she would never do such a thing by 'this heavenly light' (l.73), Emilia replies that she would not either, she would do it in the dark. Emilia is joking, trying to lighten the mood of the situation. These lines are reminiscent of Desdemona's flirtatious banter with Iago in 2.1. Desdemona may not be as innocent as she pretends to be here. Desdemona asks if Emilia would commit adultery for 'all the world' and Emilia laughs that the world would be too much for a 'small vice'. Emilia proves her wit a match for Iago's, yet until now she has avoided answering Desdemona's question directly. They are playing a game, and perhaps it is one that they have played before.

79–93 Desdemona teases Emilia a bit more. I'm sure you would not, she says, almost as if she is *daring* Emilia to take a lover. They continue to argue in a good-natured way about whether adultery can ever be entertained. They are playing at moral dilemmas. Emilia would have no hesitation in betraying Iago to make him a king, Desdemona refuses to believe that any woman would do so. Desdemona has recovered her spirits a little since the song, and for a moment everything seems normal.

94–end Emilia digresses at length about men, women and infidelity. Of course women have affairs, she says, but it is men's fault that they do. Emilia's remarks are meant to amuse Desdemona, but there might also be an undercurrent of bitterness. Does she suspect that Iago has been unfaithful? Emilia is not quite as blunt as Iago was in 2.1, but l.98 in particular is a *double entendre* that Desdemona might laugh at. If men mistreat us, Emilia says, they cannot be surprised if we mistreat them. She reflects on why men have affairs, and then points out that women have exactly the same desires and faults as men. Emilia ends with a maxim of her own: men should treat their wives well if they want them to be faithful. The speech is a performance. Emilia addresses it rhetorically to men, and perhaps Shakespeare also intended to tease the audience with these near-the-knuckle home truths.

Desdemona has enjoyed the performance and says goodbye to Emilia with a maxim of her own. The scene ends with them leaving the stage by separate exits. Though there is little in the text, both understand the significance of their parting and what is at stake. The next time Emilia sees Desdemona, in 5.2, she will be close to death.

Act V

Act V, scene i

1–10   The language is now more urgent, the pacing faster. In the last act, action has simmered, feelings have been suppressed, thoughts have festered, but now the action of the play will move swiftly to its conclusion.

Iago and Roderigo enter secretively but in haste. On Shakespeare's stage, the 'bulk' mentioned in l.1 would most likely have been one of the canopy pillars, but modern stages will have to find something for Roderigo to lurk behind where he can be seen by the audience. Roderigo will have his sword sheathed on entry, but will draw it after l.2 at Iago's instruction.

Roderigo barely seems adequate to the task of murdering Cassio. He cannot even draw his sword correctly and Iago may have to demonstrate in mime how to 'put it home' (l.2). Iago is determined to give him no time to think, and certainly no time to think for himself. Roderigo makes sure Iago will be there if everything goes wrong. Alone, Roderigo weakly admits he does not know why he is killing Cassio.

11–22 Iago boasts to the audience that he can enrage Roderigo enough to kill Cassio. He is overestimating his own abilities and Roderigo's willingness to do anything for Desdemona. Iago's speech is unexpectedly uncertain, and finishes in a different place to where it began. We are used to Iago inventing plans on the spot, but this time he changes his mind. Iago starts by saying that he does not care who dies, but as he weighs up the advantages of either of them living, he suddenly realises that he cannot afford for either of them to survive the night. Iago does not get a chance to think any further. Earlier in the play, there might have been time for more plotting, but now events are running faster than even Iago can think. Cassio is coming.

23–28 The problem, of course, is that Cassio is a much better soldier than Roderigo and so much more likely to win a fight with him. The audience already knows from Roderigo's aside that Iago has dramatically overestimated Roderigo's murderous anger. At the last moment, when it is too late to make any new plans, Iago realises he has made a serious tactical error. Both of them have to die. If later Iago silently reflects on his mistakes, this will be one of them. Iago has no choice but to act himself. Iago never acts, he does everything he can to make other people do his work for him. Now he has to take a huge risk and intervene himself to make sure that both are killed, one way or the other.

Iago is not used to blunders on this scale, and he may well not respond with his usual sure-footedness to the events as they unfold. With Cassio coming on to the stage, Iago has to make sure that he is also hidden and in a place where he can attack Cassio from behind. He may even draw his dagger right away. As soon as he sees that Cassio has defeated Roderigo, Iago rushes at Cassio, stabs him in the leg and then flees.

Why does Iago stab Cassio in the leg, when he has the opportunity to drive his dagger into Cassio's body or cut his throat? The text provides no answer to this question, but clearly Iago botches the job. Perhaps it is simply too dark for the plan to work. The audience *know* that he meant to kill Cassio, but Cassio is only wounded, he is still able to raise a cry and he will later be a witness in the play's denouement. Iago cannot have intended to stab Cassio in the leg and the action should be worked out with this in mind. To cap it all, Roderigo is still alive.

29–38 Othello watches from the shadows, delighted to see the car-
nage on the stage, muttering to himself and then talking to the absent
Desdemona. Othello does not seem to notice that neither Roderigo
nor Cassio are actually dead: both are moving, groaning, calling out
for help. This will need to make sense for the audience, even though
the scene is brief. It is very dark, but the two men are making enough
noise to raise help a few lines later. Why does Othello not hear
Cassio's 'direful' cry?

Either Othello is so wrapped up in his obsessive anger that he is
blind to what the audience can clearly see, or he is simply not close
enough to the two men to understand what has happened, and sees
only that they are on the floor covered in blood. (For example, he
could be above stage.) Alternatively, the actors could explore performance devices which play with the representation of time. Othello's
thoughts do not need to be literally contemporaneous with the length
of time it takes to say them in blank verse so, for example, the other
actors onstage could freeze as Othello speaks to signify that, within
the timeline of the play, Othello is just there for a few moments.

For Othello, the moment to kill Desdemona has come. The play
is moving breathlessly to its conclusion. His final couplet signifies
the onset of action, Desdemona's death is now as inevitable and
inescapable as the rhyme which Othello leaves the stage on.

39–47 The stage is now full of wounded men shouting, Venetians
cowering in the shadows, and Iago doing his best to exploit this
situation to mend some of the damage his earlier errors have caused.

Judging from Gratiano and Lodovico's cowardly lines, Cassio is
screaming with pain, and Roderigo may be crying as well. However,
they have no light, they can only hear noises. They decide to get help.

48–56 Iago enters and evidently has changed (perhaps into his
nightshirt). He brings with him a light. The light is not sufficient for
him to recognise (unless he pretends not to) the Venetians, but they
recognise him. They could be at different ends of the stage, shouting at
each other, as if the stage were not loud and confused enough already.

57–64 Iago goes to Cassio first, perhaps intending to finish him off,
but either because he can be seen by the Venetians, or because Cassio

cries out his name, Iago does not kill him, and instead pretends to help, calling over to the Venetians.

65–70 Iago is more fortunate with Roderigo, who shouts for help but does not recognise Iago, or at least does not call out his name until it is too late. Cassio gives Iago the prompt he needs to silence Roderigo, and he wastes no time. Iago may have failed to kill Cassio, but at least he can finally get rid of Roderigo and destroy the main witness to his plot. Just in case, Iago blots out Roderigo's death cries by shouting loudly.

71–115 Iago is beginning to regain control of the situation. Unable to kill Cassio, he presents himself instead as Cassio's saviour. He assumes authority, acting first as doctor and then as detective. He tries to piece together what has happened and, slightly waywardly, fixes the blame on Bianca. These lines revolve around Iago and his somewhat erratic attempt to determine an interpretation of events before anyone else can. Iago has been using this technique all through the play, but this time he is not as self-assured as usual. He is thinking on his feet, and he is almost too anxious to take charge. When he accuses Bianca, whom he opportunistically seizes on as the only scapegoat to hand, his ability to create his own truth out of the situation starts to look strained. Can Bianca really be implicated so blithely?

This scene should be frenetic, almost chaotic. Iago deliberately busies himself onstage, racing ahead of the Venetians as if responding to a crisis – which he is, of course, in that events have nearly run out of his control. Iago exploits the darkness to heighten the confusion and in modern theatres audiences can share this experience.

There is a lot of stage business implied in these lines. Iago strips at l.80, removing his shirt to bind Cassio's wound and handing his torch to Lodovico. Bianca enters distressed. In Shakespeare's time, the garter that Iago calls for in l.89 would most likely have been provided by the men, but for modern audiences there is no harm in Iago demanding it from Bianca. Iago takes back his light at l.95, impatiently snatching it from one of the Venetians and using it to roll over Roderigo to identify him. Again, Iago is taking charge and in so doing controlling how the event is being perceived. The text does not say who brings on the litter at l.108, nor does it particularly matter, but either the Venetians or Iago could bring on servants when they enter.

Most audiences will accept servants coming on from offstage, events are moving too swiftly for nitpicking at narrative details.

116–22   Iago stops the gentlemen and Bianca, who is distressed and apparently staring wildly (presumably after Cassio's litter). Iago has already dropped hints that he thinks Bianca guilty (l.86). What was then a sudden, opportunistic thought is now built up into a more substantial piece of mischief. We've seen Iago use these tricks before, but never so unconvincingly. This time he flits too quickly from Bianca to the Venetians, he comforts Bianca (l.116), then in the next line he tries to provoke the Venetian's suspicions about her.

123–29   Emilia's entrance gives Iago the opportunity to tell his own version of what has happened. This is as much for the Venetians' benefit as Emilia's. However, when Emilia cries for 'good Cassio' (l.126), Iago takes the opportunity to further implicate Bianca *and* smear Cassio by blaming the episode on Cassio's 'whoring' (l.127). Iago's next line is a deliberate plant, and he exploits Bianca's reaction to deepen suspicion about her even further.

130–31   Does Bianca 'shake' when she hears Iago tell his wife to find out where Cassio 'supped'? The text gives few clues: Iago says she shakes, Bianca retorts that she does not. The scene can be played either way with different effects which are worth exploring in rehearsal. If Bianca does not shake, then Iago will be trying to influence how everybody else onstage are interpreting her reactions. But it may be that Bianca does worry that she may be implicated in the attack and in l.130 is defensive, even defiant.

132–end   Emilia insults Bianca to her face and gets a frosty response. The Venetians remain silent and perhaps do not know what to make of this situation. Iago leads them out, instructing Emilia to go to Othello (which also turns out to be a critical mistake) before making his final direct address to the audience with a brief aside which reveals how shaken Iago himself is by these messy events. This is not the self-assured, even cocky Iago of earlier scenes. He is acutely conscious of the risks he is taking and how dangerous things now are for him.

Act V, scene ii

1–6 The scene begins with Othello getting ready to murder Desdemona. His words make the stage oppressively claustrophobic. Although only 22 lines long, this speech is so beautiful and terrible, violent and tender, that any number of interpretations of Othello's character can be developed out of it.

Othello's thoughts are both terrible and meandering, as if Othello cannot himself bear the full weight of what he is about to do. He is not speaking to the audience but to himself. He needs to know *why* he is doing what he is doing. What *is* the cause, which he cannot bring himself to name (l.2)? The speech is full of qualifications and conditions which seem to crash against each other. Yet I'll not make her bleed (l.3), but she must die (l.6).

7–10 Othello stumbles on a metaphor which briefly distracts him. Killing Desdemona will be like extinguishing the flame on his torch, but a torch can be relit if he changes his mind, whereas Desdemona's flame can never burn again. It is as if Othello is trying to understand what he is doing. This is also a way to delay action. He looks from the light to Desdemona, perhaps to his own hands. He seems neither angry nor murderous: now he is resolved on his action, he can reflect on its consequences in this strange, distanced way, as if he is observing himself.

10–19 Othello starts to address Desdemona, who is still asleep. Is he talking to her, is he rehearsing a speech he will make to her, or is he really trying to persuade himself? As soon as he starts to talk about Desdemona, despite what he believes she has done, he cannot help but become infatuated with her again. Talking of her rose, he cannot resist smelling it 'on the tree' (l.15) by kissing her and tasting her 'balmy breath'. This strange, sensuous moment briefly intoxicates Othello, who allows himself to kiss Desdemona again, even though he talks about killing her as he does so.

20–22 The moment moves Othello and he sheds a few tears – cruel tears, he calls them. He is already mourning Desdemona and many of his actions are typical of the behaviour of a bereaved lover rather than a would-be murderer. But Othello cannot indulge himself anymore. His kisses have drawn Desdemona from her sleep. The time has come.

23–106   The pacing of the next 60 lines will be critical to the overall performance. Played quickly, Desdemona's murder will seem cruelly inescapable, Othello utterly unstoppable; but played slowly, the scene will be agonising, Othello will be less sure of himself and looking for final provocation. In practice, a complex pacing which moves between both possibilities, though difficult to achieve, will better get to the heart of this extraordinary scene.

Othello seems to have found a way to transform revenge into a bizarre kind of duty. A clue to this attitude is in l.75, when he distinguishes between murder and sacrifice. Othello has persuaded himself that he is *sacrificing* Desdemona, that this is for her own good, hence his insistence that he only wants to kill her body, not her soul. This is a strange logic that needs to be explored carefully in rehearsal. The challenge is to recognise that Othello is no longer the raging monster he was in Act IV. He has changed. He will kill Desdemona for love, not revenge.

Desdemona still does not know why Othello is acting so violently. Although her preceding scene had a funereal atmosphere to it, she is not ready to die, nor does she expect Othello to kill her.

The audience remains informed spectators, so the whole episode is wrapped up in tragic irony. This is especially true of the first five lines (ll.23–27) when Desdemona wakes up.

The scene is, on the surface, tender. Desdemona dozily asks 'who's there?' (Othello will ask the same question in a different way at the end of this scene) and, when she sees it is Othello, she invites him to bed. Othello's behaviour does not give the waking Desdemona any reason to be alarmed, even if his next question is unexpected: he wants to know if she has prayed. Despite their arguments, Desdemona is still affectionate to Othello, especially if she notices that he has been crying. Whether Othello returns her caresses, or pushes Desdemona away, or lingers holding her before finding an excuse to let go, will depend on the actor.

26–27   Why does he ask if she has prayed (l.26)? This was never a part of the plan and will be a surprise to an audience unfamiliar with the text. Othello is surely about to kill Desdemona, now it seems he is delaying the moment. Is he really interested in her soul, or is he evading the act, or is he adding to her punishment – or all three at the same time? In l.26, Othello leaves off the last syllable of Desdemona's name, so bringing out the 'demon' implicit in it. He may even stress the last two syllables. (Note that the metre of Desdemona's next line exactly matches that of 'Desdemon' like a vague musical echo.)

28–32 Othello speaks like a soldier giving commands rather than as a lover. He offers to stand away, and perhaps does a little (Desdemona's next line could be played as if she has only half-heard his words), but he cannot sustain his matter-of-fact manner.

33–35 Othello cannot keep his brusque manner for long, and here his emotions break through. These lines can either be delivered direct to Desdemona, or they could be addressed to Desdemona rhetorically but not in a way that she is meant to hear.

Desdemona does hear enough to alarm her. Killing? What place does a word like 'kill' have in a marriage bed?

36–40 Though brief and fragmented, these lines are vital to the scene. This is a moment when tragedy could still be avoided. It is also the moment when Desdemona finally realises what perhaps she has only feared before, that Othello intends to kill her. Desdemona is not angry, nor does she try to escape; instead she is submissive and appeals to Othello's mercy.

At l.38, Othello seems to be ready to forgive her, but he is only interested in saving Desdemona's soul. Again, he seems to see what he is doing as an act of love. Desdemona clings to false hopes, but she is unsettled by Othello's inarticulate response (l.40).

41–52 Realising that Othello means to kill her, Desdemona reacts. Her lines tell us what Othello should be doing as she speaks. He rolls his eyes (l.42), he chews his bottom lip (l.48) and his body trembles (l.49).

Desdemona tells Othello that she is afraid but does not know why. Othello tells her to reflect on her sins, but Desdemona does not know what he means. How resolute is Othello? L.44 can be firm and unyielding, or quiet, or emotional, or angry. Othello is made up of all of these different psychological responses and performances can change from night to night as the actor explores these different emotional registers.

Desdemona is desperate and frantic. She repeats the word 'hope' (l.50) but Othello does not give her any.

52–55   Othello's patience has run out. He tells Desdemona to be still and she assents. This is a turning point in the scene and may warrant a pause as the two collect their thoughts. Desdemona has been asking the questions, now Othello will. She forces herself to calm down, she *needs* to hear what Othello has to say.

Othello is brooding. How does he say what is unsayable? He chooses a strategy which must startle Desdemona. He starts on the handkerchief – why did she give it to Cassio? The question seems to come out of nowhere.

56–60   Desdemona's answer is honest, but he calls her a liar and reminds her that she is about to die. Desdemona wants there to be some way out, but Othello is merely giving her a chance to save her soul, not her life. At l.58, Othello sounds like he is trying to gently coax Desdemona into confession, acting like a priest before an execution.

61–65   Othello becomes dark and fierce. The word 'choke' in l.64 foreshadows what he is about to do, something Desdemona may realise (especially if Othello matches the word with a gesture). In l.65, the word 'groan' reveals some of the depth of Othello's pain and is the closest he comes to letting Desdemona see directly into his mind.

66–82   Desdemona again begs for mercy. Othello is furious that Desdemona still denies the truth, on her deathbed, when her soul is at stake, when *I saw the handkerchief*. Desdemona is quick to answer this time: Cassio must have found it, go and get him. But Othello's next line destroys her. Cassio has already confessed – and now Othello comes as close as he dares to saying, in words, that Desdemona has committed adultery.

83–92   Desdemona never actually denies sleeping with Cassio. Instead, she says that Cassio will never admit it and when Othello tells her that Cassio is dead, she acts as if all hope is lost. Her tears make Othello even more jealous: why is she crying for Cassio?

93–100 The final lines before the murder are desperate, violent. Desdemona is begging for her life, then for a night, then for a prayer. But it is too late for all that, Othello is determined, the moment has come. With l.94, Othello pushes Desdemona to the bed. They struggle as they say the next lines. Desdemona is desperate to escape, so Othello will have to hold Desdemona down until he is in a position to kill.

How does Othello smother her? Rehearsal will discover many different ways: Othello can use a pillow, or his own hands, or some other object. In some productions, he strangles her. In developing the choreography of this action, attention should be given to its underlying eroticism as well as its violence.

The act can be quick, but will be effective if it is protracted, if Desdemona takes her time to die, if she struggles and moans, if Othello is exhausted and panting at the end of it. The audience should feel the pain of both characters, the scene should be difficult to watch, and the stage should be silent, even if only for a moment, to allow it all to sink in.

101–4 There is not long though. Emilia is calling for them at the door. Othello seems not to hear her, when he says 'what noise is this?' (l.102) he has heard Desdemona groaning. She is not dead. Now Othello is strangely methodical as he smothers her with tenderness – 'so, so'.

105–6 The act done, Othello hears Emilia's voice calling from outside the room as if becoming aware of his surroundings again. L.106 repeats l.23, but this time the question is suspicious, frightened. Othello could shout out this question, but since Emilia does not answer, this line will be better spoken as an aside.

107–23 Othello has two things on his mind: why is Emilia calling at his door so urgently, and is Desdemona actually dead? His mind flits between the two disjointedly. Ll.108–18 show this fragmentation in his mind as he tries to reason out what he should do. He rightly guesses that Emilia brings news of Cassio, but his thoughts are pulled back to Desdemona. Desdemona is no longer moaning or moving, but Othello is unsure if she is dead (we later learn that she isn't). One way to stage these lines is to allow Desdemona to move slightly when Othello is looking in the direction of Emilia's voice. Othello is hesitant and distracted as his fragmented phrases and his repetition of the phrase 'by and by' indicate. Othello shouts 'by and by' to Emilia (l.108) but is then distracted by Desdemona.

Emilia calls again and Othello admits he had forgotten to answer her, he invites her in but suddenly realises that he cannot show her Desdemona and so asks her to wait as he draws the bed curtains. Killing Desdemona has not brought Othello any peace or clarity of mind; on the contrary, he seems more broken and incapable than ever. The sense of purpose which he had when he was focused completely on Desdemona's 'sacrifice' has deserted him.

124–35   Emilia comes with news, but it is not the news that Othello was expecting. He waffles about the Moon driving men mad, and then completes Emilia's message for her. Cassio is killed. Emilia surprises him when she says that Cassio is still alive. The news stuns Othello into a sombre reflection. He is doing little to hide his guilt.

136–45   If Emilia is curious that Othello is disappointed to hear that Cassio lives, she does not have time to reflect on what this might mean, because at that moment, Desdemona cries out that she has been murdered.

Othello behaves like an inept criminal by pretending not to hear Desdemona's cry. Emilia ignores Othello and opens the bed curtains. She finds Desdemona unconscious and tries to revive her; Desdemona wakes again to insist on her innocence and then takes the blame for her death, refusing to accuse Othello whom she calls, almost on her last words, her 'kind lord'.

What does Othello do through this speech? Does Emilia notice that he under-reacts, that he does not rush to her bedside, that he does not show any concern?

146–53   Othello makes a feeble attempt to be surprised that Desdemona is dead. His first thoughts are to distance himself from the murder, but then at ll.150–51 Othello seems to change his mind. He admits that he killed Desdemona, and scorns her for telling lies on her deathbed. Why does he do this, what is the sequence of thoughts and emotions that leads to this? Othello is long past acting rationally, but even so the shift that he makes in these lines need to make sense. On one level, Othello simply cannot contain his anger, nor does he feel guilty because he believes that he has just cause. He behaves as he does, hiding Desdemona, pretending not to hear her, then asking how she was murdered, because Emilia came in too soon, before he had had a chance to think what he would do after killing Desdemona. Clearly Othello had no plan, no thought beyond this act.

154–61 Othello says to Emilia what he could not say to Desdemona: Cassio 'did top' (slept with) her (l.158). This is an important moment for Othello, the deed has been done and there is nothing to focus his rage on. Othello says these lines with Desdemona's corpse still on the bed (as it is until near the end of the scene). Does he turn his back on the body to shout at Emilia, does he stay with the body and talk to it, not looking Emilia in the eye? There are many different ways of blocking Othello but all will have the same coordinates: the bed, the body, Emilia, Othello, the light, the curtains, the door.

162–79 There is another story taking place in the same exchange. Emilia is startled to hear that her husband has put Othello up to this. She may have suspected Iago before, but the revelation nonetheless shocks her almost into silence: she can only repeat 'my husband' as if unable to take in the full significance of what Othello is saying. Emilia, not Othello, is the focus of this exchange.

With l.179, Othello drives his point home to this foolish woman who does not seem to understand: Iago told him, honest, *honest* Iago.

180–93 Emilia shows her courage now and speaks back, defending Desdemona, condemning Iago and insulting Othello. This is too much for Othello, who is already on the edge of violence. He draws his sword, but Emilia ignores him. Othello steadies himself, warning Emilia not to provoke him any further. Othello does not know what he is capable of, or how far he will go, in this temper. Emilia will not be silenced. She rebukes Othello, mocks his sword and calls for help.

194–220 Othello does not kill Emilia, in fact he lets her cry out for help. He has no appetite for more murder. He could justify

Desdemona's sacrifice to himself and for a while, Othello seems to think everyone else will forgive him when they understand what Desdemona has done. Montano, Gratiano and Iago respond, all must come at the same time (but not necessarily from the same place).

Iago will immediately notice Desdemona and Othello and will guess at what has happened. He will be less prepared for Emilia's accusations. Montano and Gratiano will take longer to understand this confusing situation – especially as Emilia ignores them and attacks Iago, arguing with him for 20 lines. Emilia does what no one else has done in the play, she calls Iago a liar. So forceful is she that Iago can hardly get a word in, but he may be reluctant to speak anyway. He is not in control of this situation, and if he hid behind innuendo and pretence before, now he must give plain answers and tell bold lies.

Iago tells Emilia to be quiet, but she will not be ruled, not anymore. She continues to rail at Iago and when she points to Desdemona, and the men 'stare' (as Othello tells us) horrified and astonished, her words are paralysed into a repetition of the word 'villainy', flung out as a curse and an accusation.

221–32   Iago calls her mad and tries to send her away, but Emilia takes control of herself, ignores Iago and speaks directly to Montano and Gratiano, half-apologising for her behaviour before turning back to Iago and refusing to move.

Othello falls on the bed, moaning inarticulately. Something provokes this crisis, but it may not be anything that Iago or Emilia have said. Some other drama has been playing out as they've been speaking and Othello is finally overcome. What does he do when he 'falls on the bed' (a stage direction only in the Quarto)? Does he hold Desdemona, or address her, or kiss her? Or does he ignore her? Is he crying out of anger, grief or fear?

Emilia immediately becomes his accuser, like a chorus commenting on the action, but Othello bites back, his reaction almost a howl. She was *foul*, he roars, as he rises from the bed. He then turns to admit to Gratiano that he has killed his niece.

233–38   Gratiano and Montano are astonished. Shakespeare slips in a very minor plot point that will probably escape most audiences: Brabantio, Desdemona's father, has died.

239–46   Othello spells out his case soberly. For a moment, the play seems to have returned to the situation which concluded Act I, when all Othello had to do was explain himself and charm his audience with a story which would set everything right. This story soon comes apart.

247–55   Both Emilia and Iago react when Othello mentions the handkerchief. Emilia is horrified, as she realises what Iago has done with the napkin she found. Iago tries to stop her speaking, but Emilia is determined to have her say. She does not immediately tell Othello and the others what she knows, but instead taunts Iago. Iago betrays himself by drawing his sword, but Gratiano (and probably Montano as well) hold him back.

256–77   Emilia is defiant. So confident is she now that she insults the 'dull Moor' before telling the true story of the handkerchief. In the next ten lines Emilia and Iago shout at each other, and it may be that Iago is still restrained by Gratiano (or Gratiano blocks Iago's path). Othello says nothing at first, as if this is a truth too much for him to bear, but he does not brood long: his attack on Iago is sudden.

Somehow Iago manages to evade Othello and in the confusion Iago stabs Emilia from behind. How this piece of action is staged is up to the actors, but Montano will have a part in restraining and disarming Othello because he has his dagger a few lines later. Emilia falls and someone onstage will carry her over to the bed to lie next to Desdemona. Iago flees, and Gratiano is left bewildered.

Montano gives Othello's dagger to Gratiano and orders him to guard the door outside. For a moment the quiet stage presents a strange picture: Desdemona murdered, Emilia dying, Othello destroyed.

278–95   Alone and lost in despair, Othello ponders his inadequacy. He couldn't even kill Iago. Does Othello notice Emilia dying on the bed, plaintively singing the song Desdemona had earlier taught her? Emilia chides him one last time. Does Othello listen? If he does, he says nothing as his thoughts turn to more violence.

This short interlude in the scene is worth spending some time developing. Othello is alone but we do not hear his thoughts, we are not allowed into his mind. Instead we see the consequences of his actions.

Remembering he has another sword, Othello is suddenly a man of action again, searching his room for the place where it was hidden. As soon as he finds it, he calls for Gratiano, who is an old man, hardly fit to be a guard. He enters still holding Othello's original dagger, but nervous all the same. He should be – Othello has found an old sword and is standing with it, showing it to him.

296–308   Othello speaks to the terrified Gratiano at length. Othello turns abruptly from Gratiano to Desdemona and then his words dissolve into inarticulate sobs. Othello shows Gratiano his sword. Othello could kill a man without a weapon, so Gratiano will be particularly conscious of the danger Othello poses as he studies the weapon in his hand, as his thoughts meander, as he turns to face the woman he has just killed.

Othello is barely making any sense, but what he says matters less than how he says it. His first six lines seem to be addressed to the sword he has found. His words recall his earlier tale of the handkerchief: Othello likes to endow objects with power, and seeing the sword takes him back to a time when he understood what he was and what he could do. At l.296, Othello appears to threaten Gratiano, but Othello then tells him to not be afraid before dwelling darkly on his 'journey's end', which he says whilst studying the various parts of his sword. Gratiano retreats, dismayed. Othello is lost, he threatens no one but himself.

Why has Othello called Gratiano in? More to the point, why is Shakespeare stretching out the drama? In a play which is relatively fast-moving, and in an act which is full of urgent action, these last lines are interminable. In other plays, the action would be done by now and the audience would be collecting their coats: Iago would be dead, Othello would have killed himself, Lodovico would have given a final speech. Instead, the action drags on without clear purpose. In narrative terms, there is nothing left to achieve, but this procrastination does have another purpose. Shakespeare refuses to let the audience off the hook, he forces them to endure the unendurable. Gratiano is there to represent the audience onstage: his dismay, his horror, reflects to the audience an image of themselves as Shakespeare imagines them to be. And through all of this, the bodies of Desdemona and Emilia on the bed are a constant reminder of what has happened.

308–18   Othello now turns to Desdemona. When he asks where he could go, he means this as a rhetorical question to show Gratiano that he has no need to escape: but having asked the question, he is drawn to Desdemona's body. Where else could he go but to Desdemona? But he cannot go there anymore. He cannot go there in life, in death he will be punished in hell. Othello's words grow more graphic, more self-flagellating, before he breaks down. The audience's attention will be fully on Othello, so Gratiano only needs to be, like them, a witness to Othello's despair. Othello may throw himself on the bed, he may clutch at Desdemona as he punishes himself – or he may not feel worthy of even touching her.

319–80   There is some action at the start when Othello tries to kill Iago: he fails and is disarmed. Even at the last Othello is a failure. The rest of these lines are largely expository and may even be cut: the audience knows all this anyway. Iago claims a final victory of his own by refusing to talk, so Iago – one of Shakespeare's most verbose characters – ends the play in silence. This is a great opportunity for the actor playing Iago, he can develop his own ending for the character. How does Iago react to Roderigo's letters, Othello's torment?

381–end   Othello's final speech returns some dignity and bearing to the character. For the first time since Act III, we hear the Othello who charmed Brabantio and Desdemona. Othello's anger and grief have been emptied. When he stabs himself at the end of the speech, he does so in a business-like way, as if he were punishing a subordinate, and it is as a lover rather than as a monster that he dies, kissing Desdemona. Has Iago won or lost, what does he think when he looks on this scene? He has engineered their deaths, but they are still together as Lodovico draws the curtain on them, gives instructions to torture Iago, and readies himself to tell Othello's story.

3   The Play's Intellectual
and Cultural Contexts

The sources and primary documents below have been selected to provoke insights into Shakespeare's treatment of race and gender in *Othello*. They should provoke productive discussions in rehearsals and workshops. However, understanding the context of the play should not foreclose creative interpretation of the play; on the contrary, if used right, these works, written by people for whom *Othello* was a contemporary or near-contemporary play, can be used dynamically with the text to generate new ideas for performance. Because *Othello* is unusually enmeshed in a very complex and emerging cultural context, these documents can only serve as an introduction to the play's intellectual and cultural contexts. I begin with two of Shakespeare's sources to shed light on the material with which Shakespeare crafted *Othello*. Following that, extracts from the anonymous play *Lust's Dominion* and Shakespeare's own early play, *Titus Andronicus*, present different ways in which the Shakespearean stage represented race. Thomas Rymer's diatribe against *Othello*, discussed as a work of criticism in Chapter 6, is reproduced here to illustrate how *Othello* could provoke extreme reactions nearly a century after it was written. This section concludes with an extract from one of the many journals of travels in Africa published during the period, to give some insight into how the early modern mind encountered (physically and imaginatively) other races.

From Giraldi Cinthio, *Gli Hecatommithi* (1565, this excerpt is adapted from a translation by John Edward Taylor, 1855)

In Venice there once lived a brave Moor who was honoured by the Venetian Signoria for his bravery and prowess in battle in the service of the Republic. A virtuous and beautiful lady called Disdemona fell in love with the Moor because of his courage; and, overcome by Disdemona's beauty and noble character, he also fell in love with her; and their desire was so strong that, although the lady's parents tried as hard as they could to persuade her to take another husband, she agreed to marry the Moor; and they lived so harmoniously and peacefully in Venice that they never said any words to each other which were not loving and kind.

[...]

In the army there was an Ensign, who was good-looking but had a twisted nature. He was respected by the Moor, who did not know about his wickedness; for he covered with proud and brave words the lurking malice in his heart, ...

[...]

The wicked Ensign, ignoring the pledges of his own marriage and the friendship, fidelity and obligation which he owed the Moor, fell passionately in love with Disdemona, and turned all his thoughts to achieve his conquest; yet he did not dare to declare his feelings openly, fearing that, should the Moor see it, he would at once kill him. He therefore tried in various ways, and with secret guile, to betray his passion to the lady; but she, whose every wish was directed at the Moor, did not think about the Ensign more than she would any other man, and all the schemes he used to win her love had no more effect that if he had not tried them. But the Ensign thought that the reason for his lack of success was that Disdemona was really in love with the Captain of the troop; and the love which he had for the lady now changed into bitter hate, and, having failed in his plans, he turned his mind to plot the murder of the Captain and to turn the Moor against Disdemona. After turning over in his mind various plans, all equally hateful, he at last decided to accuse her of adultery with the Captain. But knowing the special love the Moor had for Disdemona, and the friendship he had for the Captain, he was keenly aware that, unless he came up with a brilliant way to deceive the Moor, it would be impossible to make him give any credence to either accusation; so he resolved to wait until time and circumstance were right for his foul plan to succeed.

Not long after this, the Moor stripped the Captain of his rank for fighting with and wounding a soldier of the guard. Disdemona was very upset about this and tried again and again to persuade the Moor to reinstate the Captain. The Moor confided to the Ensign that Disdemona was talking about this to him so much that he worried he would be obliged to accept the Captain back into service. This was enough for the Ensign to act and he begun to spin his web of intrigue. 'Perhaps,' he said, 'the lady Disdemona has a good reason to favour the Captain.'

'Why?' said the Moor.

'I don't want to come between a man and his wife,' replied the Ensign, 'but let your eyes see what they will see.'

[…]

The Moor, seeing how earnestly his wife pleaded for the Captain, began to guess what the Ensign meant. So, wrapped up in melancholy, the Moor sought out the villain to get him to speak more candidly about what he knew. Then the Ensign, who was determined to ruin the unhappy lady, after having pretended to be reluctant to say anything that might upset the Moor, finally made a show of giving in to his pleas, and said, 'I can't deny it pains me to the soul to be compelled to tell you something that will be harder to hear than any other grief; but since you insist, and that the regard I have for your honor compels me to confess the truth, I will no longer refuse to satisfy your questions and my duty. You must know, then, that your lady is upset by the Captain's disgrace for no other reason than because she enjoys his company whenever he comes to your house, and especially since she has developed a repugnance for your blackness.'

These words cut straight to the Moor's heart; but in order to hear more (now that he believed the truth of what the Ensign had told him) he replied, with a fierce eye, 'By heavens, I can barely hold my hand from ripping out your tongue, which so boldly dares to slander my wife!'

[…]

Then the Moor, full of indignation and anguish, said, 'Either make my eyes witness of what you have said or on your life I'll make you wish you had been born without a tongue.'

[…]

Disdemona often used to go, as I have already said, to visit the Ensign's wife, and stayed with her for a good part of the day. Now, the Ensign noticed that she had with her a handkerchief, which he knew the Moor had given her, finely embroidered in the Moorish fashion, and which was precious to Disdemona, and to the Moor. Then he came up with a plan to secretly steal the handkerchief, and so set the trap for her downfall.

[…]

The evil Ensign, taking advantage of a suitable opportunity, went to the Captain of the troop, and cunningly placed the handkerchief at the head of his bed without his discovering the trick until the following morning, when, on his getting out of bed, the handkerchief fell upon the floor, and he stepped on it.

[…]

The Ensign […] arranged it so that he could talk to the Captain whilst the Moor was hidden where he could see and hear them as they spoke. And as he talked to him about every subject apart from that of Disdemona, he constantly laughed out loud and pretended to be astonished with various movements with his head and hands, as if he were listening to an incredible story. As soon as the Moor saw the Captain leave, he went up to the Ensign to find out what he had said to him. The Ensign, after being pressed hard, said at last, 'He has concealed nothing from me and has told me that he has been in the habit of visiting your wife whenever you've been away from home, and that the last time she gave him the handkerchief which you gave to her when you married.'

From Geoffrey Fenton, *Certain Tragical Discourses* (1567; based on Matteo Bandello's *Novelle*, 1554)

But alas the unfortunate Lady, brewed hear the broth of her own bane, and spun the thread of her own destruction, for falling now unhapply into the malice of her destiny, thinking nothing less then of the secret ambush of mortal treason her husband had laid for her, went unhapply to bed with him the same night, where for his part, prefering in his face a show of feigned contentment (& consolation to the eye), he forced a further quiet of mind by the joy he imagined in the act he meant to do, but chiefly for that he had devised how the innocent Lady (through the rage of his villainy) should be forced to an effect of her promisse, for the speedy execution wherof, they had not been long in bed together, but he rose from her, feigning a desire to perform the necessity of nature in the closet or chamber of secrets, his errand indeed being to fetch his dagger, which (without making her privy) he conveyed under the bolster of his bed, beginning even then to prefer a preamble afore the part he meant to play. For, falling from his former complaints of sickness, he retired into terms of extreme frenzy and madness, braying out such groans and sighs of hideous disposition, with howling, crying, and foaming at the mouth, like one possessed with an evil spirit, that who had seen his often change of colour and complexion in his face, his ghastly regards arguing ententes of desperation, and his eyes (flaming with fury) sunk into his head, with the order of his passion every way, might easily have judged the desire of his heart to be of no small importance, and the thing he went about neither common nor commendable. Wherein he was assisted with three enemies of diverse dispositions, love, jealousy, and death: the least of the which is sufficient of himself to make a man chafe in his harness, and take away the courage of his heart in the midst of the combat. For the one presented a certain fear by reason of the horror of the act; the other sewed (as it were) for an abstinence, or at least a moderation, of the cruelty he had commenced against his innocent wife; but the third, being the beginner of all, and exceeding the rest in power, would not dismiss him from the stage till he had played the uttermost act of his malicious tragedy.

Mark here (good ladies) the desolation of this unfortunate gentlewoman, and dispose yourselves to tears on the behalf of her distress. Wherein, certainly, you have no less reason to help to bewail her wretched chance, then just occasion to join in general exclamation against the detestable act of her tyrannous husband; who, disclaiming even now his former state and condition of a man, retires into the habit of a monster, and cruel enemy to nature; and in converting the virtue of his former love, and remembrance of the sundry pleasures he had heretofore received of his dear and loving wife, into present rage and unnatural fury (far exceeding the savage and brutish manner of the tiger, lion . . . bred in the deserts of Africa, the common Norse of monsters and creatures cruel without reason) whetting his teeth for the terrible suggestion of the devil, who at the instant put into his hand the dagger; wherewith, after he had embraced and kissed her, in such sort as Judas kissed our Lord the same night he betrayed him, he saluted her with ten or twelve estockados [stabs], one in the neck . . . another in diverse parts of her body, renewing the conflict with no less number of blows in her head and arms; and because no part should escape free from the stroke of his malice, he visited her white and tender legs, with no less rage and fury then the rest. Wherewith, beholding in her diverse undoubted arguments of death, began the like war with himself, using the same mean and ministers with his own hands, enbrewed yet with the blood of his innocent wife; showing (notwithstanding this horrible part and act of despair) diverse and sundry signs of special gladness and pleasure in his face, wherein he continued till the last and extreme gasp of life, chiefly for that he saw him accompanied to death with her, whom he was not able to leave behinde him . . . who, being overcharged (as you have heard) with the number of wounds, the violence whereof (prevailing far above the resistance of life) did press her so much with the hasty approach of death, that the want of breath abridged her secret shrift and confession to God, with less leisure to yield her innocent soul (with humble prayer) into the hands of her Redeemer, and commend the forgiveness of her sins to the benefit of his mercy. Only she had respite (with great ado to speak) to give order that her body might be laid in the tomb of her first husband, Signeur Barzo.

But the cursed and execrable Albanoys (so wholly possessed with the devil that the gift of grace was denied him) abhorred to the last minute of his life the remembrance of repentance; for, laughing (as it were) at the foulness of the fact even until life left him senseless and void of breath, he commended his carcass to the greedy jaws of ravenous wolves, serving also as a fit prey for the venomous serpents and other creeping worms of the earth, and his soul to the reprobate society of Judas and Cain, with other of the infernal crew.

From Anon., *Lust's Dominion,* or *The Lascivious Queen* (2.2; edited by Mary Ellen Cacheado)

Enter the two Moors

BOTH   My Lord.
ELEAZAR   Nearer, so; silence;
  Hang both your greedy ears upon my lips,
  Let them devour my speech, suck in my breath;
  And in who lets it break prison, here's his death.
  This night the Cardinal shall be murdered.
BOTH   Where?
ELEAZAR   And to fill up a grave Philip dies.
BOTH   Where?
ELEAZAR   Here.
BOTH   By whom?
ELEAZAR   By thee! And, slave, by thee.
  Have you hearts and hands to execute?
BOTH   Here's both.
1 MOOR   He dies, were he my father.
ELEAZAR   Ho away?
  Stay, go, go, stay, see me no more till night;
  Your cheeks are black, let not your souls look white.
BOTH   Till night.
ELEAZAR   Till night; a word: the Mother Queen
  Is trying if she can with fire of gold
  Warp the green consciences of two covetous friars,
  To preach abroad Philip's bastardy.

1 MOOR   His bastardy? Who was his father?
ELEAZAR   Who?
Search for these friars, hire them to work with you;
Their holy callings will approve the fact
Most good and meritorious, sin shines clear,
When her black face religions mask doth wear.

From William Shakespeare, *Titus Andronicus* (5.1)

Enter a Goth leading of Aron with his child in his Armes

SECOND GOTH   Renowned Lucius, from our troops I stray'd
To gaze upon a ruinous Monastery;
And, as I earnestly did fix mine eye
Upon the wasted building, suddenly
I heard a child cry underneath a wall.
I made unto the noise, when soon I heard
The crying babe controll'd with this discourse:
'Peace, tawny slave, half me and half thy Dam!
Did not thy hue bewray whose brat thou art,
Had nature lent thee but thy mother's look,
Villain, thou mightst have been an emperor:
But where the bull and cow are both milk-white,
They never do beget a coal-black calf.
Peace, villain, peace!' Even thus he rates the babe,
'For I must bear thee to a trusty Goth
Who, when he knows thou art the Empress' babe,
Will hold thee dearly for thy mother's sake.'
With this, my weapon drawn, I rush'd upon him,
Surprised him suddenly, and brought him hither,
To use as you think needful of the man.
LUCIUS   O worthy Goth, this is the incarnate devil
That robb'd Andronicus of his good hand;
This is the pearl that pleased your Empress' eye,
And here's the base fruit of his burning lust.
Say, wall-eyed slave, whither wouldst thou convey
This growing image of thy fiend-like face?
Why dost not speak? What, deaf? Not a word?
A halter, soldiers, hang him on this tree.

    And by his side his fruit of bastardy.

AARON   Touch not the boy; he is of royal blood.

LUCIUS   Too like the sire for ever being good.
    First hang the child, that he may see it sprawl;
    A sight to vex the father's soul withal.
    Get me a ladder.

AARON   Lucius, save the child,
    And bear it from me to the Empress.
    If thou do this, I'll show thee wondrous things,
    That highly may advantage thee to hear:
    If thou wilt not, befall what may befall,
    I'll speak no more but 'Vengeance rot you all!'

LUCIUS   Say on: an if it please me which thou speak'st
    Thy child shall live, and I will see it nourish'd.

AARON   An if it please thee? Why, assure thee, Lucius,
    'Twill vex thy soul to hear what I shall speak;
    For I must talk of murders, rapes and massacres,
    Acts of black night, abominable deeds,
    Complots of mischief, treason, villanies
    Ruthful to hear, yet piteously perform'd:
    And this shall all be buried by my death,
    Unless thou swear to me my child shall live.

LUCIUS   Tell on thy mind; I say thy child shall live.

AARON   Swear that he shall, and then I will begin.

LUCIUS   Who should I swear by? Thou believest no god:
    That granted, how canst thou believe an oath?

AARON   What if I do not? As, indeed, I do not;
    Yet, for I know thou art religious
    And hast a thing within thee called conscience,
    With twenty popish tricks and ceremonies,
    Which I have seen thee careful to observe,
    Therefore I urge thy oath; for that I know
    An idiot holds his bauble for a God
    And keeps the oath which by that God he swears,
    To that I'll urge him: therefore thou shalt vow
    By that same God, what God soe'er it be,
    That thou adorest and hast in reverence,
    To save my boy, to nourish and bring him up;
    Or else I will discover nought to thee.

LUCIUS   Even by my god I swear to thee I will.

AARON   First know thou, I begot him on the Empress.

LUCIUS   O most insatiate and luxurious woman.
AARON   Tut, Lucius, this was but a deed of charity
   To that which thou shalt hear of me anon.
   'Twas her two sons that murder'd Bassianus;
   They cut thy sister's tongue and ravish'd her
   And cut her hands and trimm'd her as thou saw'st.
LUCIUS   O detestable villain! Call'st thou that trimming?
AARON   Why, she was wash'd and cut and trimm'd, and 'twas
   Trim sport for them that had the doing of it.
LUCIUS   O barbarous, beastly villains, like thyself!
AARON   Indeed, I was their tutor to instruct them:
   That codding spirit had they from their mother,
   As sure a card as ever won the set;
   That bloody mind, I think, they learn'd of me,
   As true a dog as ever fought at head.
   Well, let my deeds be witness of my worth.
   I train'd thy brethren to that guileful hole
   Where the dead corpse of Bassianus lay:
   I wrote the letter that thy father found
   And hid the gold within the letter mention'd,
   Confederate with the Queen and her two sons:
   And what not done, that thou hast cause to rue,
   Wherein I had no stroke of mischief in it?
   I play'd the cheater for thy father's hand,
   And, when I had it, drew myself apart
   And almost broke my heart with extreme laughter:
   I pry'd me through the crevice of a wall
   When, for his hand, he had his two sons' heads;
   Beheld his tears, and laugh'd so heartily,
   That both mine eyes were rainy like to his:
   And when I told the Empress of this sport,
   She swooned almost at my pleasing tale,
   And for my tidings gave me twenty kisses.
FIRST GOTH   What, canst thou say all this, and never blush?
AARON   Ay, like a black dog, as the saying is.
LUCIUS   Art thou not sorry for these heinous deeds?
AARON   Ay, that I had not done a thousand more.
   Even now I curse the day and yet, I think,
   Few come within the compass of my curse,
   Wherein I did not some notorious ill,
   As kill a man, or else devise his death,
   Ravish a maid, or plot the way to do it,

Accuse some innocent and forswear myself,
Set deadly enmity between two friends,
Make poor men's cattle break their necks;
Set fire on barns and haystacks in the night,
And bid the owners quench them with their tears:
Oft have I digg'd up dead men from their graves,
And set them upright at their dear friends' doors,
Even when their sorrows almost were forgot;
And on their skins, as on the bark of trees,
Have with my knife carved in Roman letters,
'Let not your sorrow die, though I am dead.'
But I have done a thousand dreadful things
As willingly as one would kill a fly,
And nothing grieves me heartily indeed
But that I cannot do ten thousand more.

LUCIUS   Bring down the devil for he must not die
So sweet a death as hanging presently.

AARON   If there be Devils, would I were a Devil,
To live and burn in everlasting fire,
So I might have your company in hell,
But to torment you with my bitter tongue.

LUCIUS   Sirs, stop his mouth, and let him speak no more.

From Thomas Rymer, *Othello: A Bloody Farce* (1693)

What ever rubs or difficulty may stick on the Bark, the Moral, sure, of this Fable is very instructive.

First, this may be a caution to all Maidens of Quality how, without their Parents consent, they run away with Blackamoors.

Secondly, this may be a warning to all good Wives, that they look well to their Linen.

Thirdly, this may be a lesson to Husbands, that before their Jealousy be Tragical, the proofs may be Mathematical.

Cinthio affirms that she was not overcome by a Womanish Appetite, but by the Virtue of the Moor. It must be a good-natur'd Reader that takes Cinthio's word in this case, tho' in a Novel. Shakespears, who is account-able both to the Eyes, and to the Ears, And to convince the very heart of an Audience, shows that Desdemona was won, by hearing Othello talk,

OTHELLO: I spoke of most disastrous chances,
of Moving accidents, by flood and field;

> of hair-breadth scapes i' th' imminent deadly breach;
> of being taken by the insolent foe;
> and sold to slavery: of my redemption thence;
> and portents in my Travels History:
> wherein of Antars vast, and Desarts idle,
> rough Quarries, Rocks, and Hills, whose heads touch heaven,
> It was my hint to speak, such was my process:
> and of the Cannibals that each others eat:
> the Anthropophagi, and men whose heads
> do grow beneath their shoulders . . .   (1.iii.134–45)

This was the Charm, this was the philtre, the love-powder that took the Daughter of this Noble Venetian. This was sufficient to make the Black-amoor White, and reconcile all, tho' there had been a Cloven-foot into the bargain.

Shakespeare in this Play calls 'em the supersubtle Venetians. Yet examine throughout the Tragedy there is nothing in the noble Desdemona, that is not below any Country Chamber-maid with us. And the account he gives of their Nobelmen and Senate, can only be calculated for the latitude of Gotham.

The Character of that State is to employ strangers in their Wars; but shall a Poet thence fancy that they will set a Negro to be their General; or trust a Moor to defend them against the Turk? With us a Black-amoor might rise to be a Trumpeter; but Shakespeare would not have him less than a Lieutenant-General. With us a Moor might marry some little drab, or Small-coal Wench: Shakespeare would provide him the Daughter and Heir of some great Lord, or Privy-Councellor: and all the Town should reckon it a very suitable match: yet the English are not bred up with that hatred and aversion to the Moors, as are the Venetians, who suffer by a perpetual Hostility from them. *Littora littoribus contraris.* Nothing is more odious in Nature than an improbable lie; And, certainly, never was any Play fraught, like this of Othello, with improbabilities.

From Leo Africanus, *Geographical History of Africa* (1600)

Of Ileusugaghen a towne of Hea

This town is situated upon the top of a certain high mountain which is distant eight miles to the South of Hadecchis: it consisteth of about two hundred families: and by the foot of the hill runneth a small river. Here are no gardens at all, nor yet any trees which bear fruit: the reason whereof is (as I suppose) because the inhabitants are such slothfull and grosse people, that they regard nothing but their barley and their oil. They are at continual war with their next neighbours, which is performed with such monstrous bloodshed and manslaughter, that they deserve rather the name of beasts than of men. They have neither judges, priests, nor lawyers, to prescribe any form of living among them, or to govern their common-wealth: wherefore justice and honesty is quite banished out of their habitations. Those mountains are altogether destitute of fruits: how be it they abound greatly with honey, which serveth the inhabitants both for food, and for merchandise to sell in the neighbour-countries. And because they know not what service to put their wax unto, they cast it forth, together with the other excrements of honey. The said town of Ileusugaghen hath a very small and narrow chapel, which will scarce contain a hundred persons, whither notwithstanding the people do so slowly resort, that they need not to have any greater; so much do they neglect religion and piety. Whensoever they go abroad, they carry a dagger or a javelin about with them: and you shall often hear of the slaughter of some one or other of their citizens. No people under heaven can be more wicked, treacherous, or lewdly addicted, then this people is.

I remember that I myself went once thither with a Seriffo or Mahumetan priest (who made challenge unto the government of Hea) to the end that we might arbitrate certain strifes and contentions: for it were incredible to report, what cruell wars, partly for murders, and partly for robberies, were practised among them. But because the Seriffo had brought no lawyers with him, nor any judges to decide controversies, he would needs, that I should take that office upon me. Immediately the townsmen come flocking about us: one complaines that his neighbour hath slain eight of his kindred and family; his neighbour on the contrary allegdeth, that the former had slain ten of his family; wherefore, according to the ancient custom, he demandeth to have a sum of money given him. For (saith he) there is some recompense due unto me, since ten of my people have been slain, and but eight of this my neighbours. Whereunto the other replied that the said ten persons were justly slain, because they went about by violence to dispossess him of a certain piece of ground which his father had left him by inheritance; but, that his eight were murdered only for unjust revenge, against all equity and law. With these and such like frivolous allegations we spent that whole day, neither could we decide any one controversy. About midnight we saw a great throng of people meet in the market-place, who made there such a bloody and horrible conflict, that the sight thereof would have affrighted any man, were he never so hard-hearted. Wherefore the said Seriffo fearing least those lewd varlets would make some treacherous conspiracy against him, and thinking it better to depart thence immediately, then to expect the conclusion of that fray, we took our journey from that place to a town called Aghilinghighil.

4 Key Productions and Performances

Othello was once one of the most important and frequently staged of Shakespeare's plays. For three centuries, the play dominated the English stage to such an extent that it would be possible to tell the story of theatre's development from the Jacobean to the Victorian eras solely through *Othello*'s production history. Richard Burbage, Thomas Betterton, David Garrick, Edmund Kean, William Charles Macready and Henry Irving were all celebrated for either Iago or Othello (often both). *Othello* was among the first plays to be staged after the Restoration, and may have been the first play to cast women rather than men. In an age when it was common practice to adapt Shakespeare's plays (sometimes drastically), *Othello* tended to be performed in its original version. Today, despite the high level of critical and educational interest in *Othello*, there are fewer opportunities than ever to see the play in performance.

One reason for this is that the racial politics of casting Othello discourages many theatre companies. Until the end of the 20th century, Othello was usually played by a leading white actor wearing 'blackface' make-up to make him look either African or Middle Eastern. Blackface theatre was immensely popular in the 19th century when minstrelsy shows were at their height, but even in the 1840s the famous abolitionist Frederick Douglass (himself a former slave) was writing scathingly about the racism inherent in the practice of white men pretending to be black (Lott, 1995, pp. 15–37). The African-American singer and political activist Paul Robeson broke new ground with his record-breaking run as Othello on Broadway in the 1940s, and since then it has become normal for Othello to be played by black actors, and politically dubious for white actors to take on the role. Laurence Olivier blacked-up for his landmark

Othello at the National Theatre in the 1960s, and other white actors since Olivier have attempted the role, among them Brewster Mason, Donald Sinden and Paul Scofield, but by the early 1980s the practice was so controversial that the BBC faced hostile criticism for casting Anthony Hopkins, who blacked-up for the role (see Chapter 5). The last significant white actor to play Othello was Patrick Stewart for the Shakespeare Theatre in Washington D.C. in 1997. In an original twist to the play's performance history, Stewart did not black-up; instead, as a gesture to the underlying race politics that now haunt the play, he and director Jude Kelly cast black actors for Iago, Desdemona and the rest of the Venetian characters. Stewart called this 'photo-negative' casting, but his remains a one-off experiment.

The question of whether black actors *should* play the part has also become a contentious issue which is best summed up by the African-American actor Hugh Quarshie:

> I am left with a nagging doubt: if a black actor plays Othello does he not risk making racial stereotypes seem legitimate and true? When a black actor plays a role written for a white actor in black make-up and for a predominantly white audience, does he not encourage the white way, or rather the wrong way, of looking at black men, namely that black men, or 'Moors', are over-emotional, excitable and unstable, thereby vindicating Iago's statement, 'These Moors are changeable in their wills' (I.3.346)? Of all the parts in the canon, perhaps Othello is the one which should most definitely not be played by a black actor.
>
> (Quarshi, 1999, p. 5)

Quarshie's answer was to move the goalposts. *Othello* may be a 'seriously flawed play', he wrote, but with the right approach, the character could be played as 'a black man responding to racism, not giving a pretext to it'. Quarshie has played Othello himself, so he writes from experience about the cultural difficulty – and opportunity – that the role presents. Quarshie's 'nagging doubt', shared by many actors, has thrown a shadow over *Othello*'s recent performance history.

A survey of productions in the subsidised British theatres reveals how far *Othello* has moved away from the centre of the theatrical canon. There were nine major productions at the Royal Shakespeare Company (RSC) (including the years when it was called the Shakespeare Memorial Theatre) between 1945 and 1985, all staged in the largest available theatre spaces. Several of these productions were so successful that they were subsequently restaged. By contrast, between 1985 (when Ben Kingsley took the lead in a production directed by Terry Hands) and 2010, *Othello* has only once been staged in the main house when Ray Fearon played Othello for a production directed by Michael Attenbrough in 1999. There have been several notable productions in these years which give the impression of a sustained tradition of playing the play with major actors, but all have been staged in the RSC's smaller theatres such as the Swan, or reserved for the RSC's touring venues. The most critically successful production in this period, directed by Trevor Nunn in 1989, was played in the RSC's tiny studio theatre, The Other Place. The Royal National Theatre has not played *Othello* on its largest stage, the Olivier, since Peter Hall's 1980 production. Recent *Othellos* have attracted big name stars such as Ewan McGregor and Lenny Henry, but these productions have also been played in small studio theatres or taken on tour. The days when *Othello* dominated the London stage are long past.

By becoming less central to the Western theatrical canon, *Othello* has become a play which directors and actors feel able to take more risks with. *Othello* was once a vehicle for star actors to show off their physical and emotional range. Today, the play is more likely to be staged in a way that addresses present-day identity politics. In this chapter, I will look more closely at how Robeson and Olivier defined different paths for *Othello* in the modern period. I will then survey productions which, by taking *Othello* into smaller theatres, have found in the play a new urgency for modern audiences.

'Not in hate, but in honour': Paul Robeson

Looking at any spread of photographs of 20th-century Othellos, the difference between black and blacked-up actors is striking. There is Frederick Valk, arms heroically outstretched, his large body covered in black make-up in 1942 for the Old Vic; Ralph Richardson, lean and sinister with an exotic goatee beard standing over Desdemona with a curved Turkish blade in 1937 (also at the Old Vic); Johnston Forbes-Robertson peeping through the curtains, a thin coating of black-face doing nothing to conceal his Caucasian ethnicity, gold earrings hinting at an unlikely exoticism in 1913 (Drury Lane). And then, with a quiet, dignified force, modernity seems to break in with photographs of Paul Robeson, the black singer, actor and activist who played the role several times over 20 years. He is a large man, a giant next to Peggy Ashcroft's striking but fragile Desdemona in 1930 at the Savoy. When he puts a hand around her neck, to lift her face up lovingly (but also perhaps to strangle her) his hands stretch to the back of her head. He could kill her in a moment. His eyes are intense, sad; his face beautiful, his costume plain rather than exotic. Against Robeson's Othello, all blacked-up Othellos look artificial and mannered.

Robeson was not the first black actor to play Othello. In 1821 James Hewlett led a group of amateur black actors in New York in a production of *Othello* at an improvised theatre space which had to be closed because of fears of a public disturbance. The presiding magistrate apparently made Hewlett and his company promise never to play Shakespeare again (Speaight, 1973, p. 71). America was not ready for a black Othello. England was no more tolerant, but the race issue did not cut to the core of political stability in quite the same way as it did in America, where the slavery issue would eventually lead to civil war. Consequently, the African-American actor Ira Aldridge was able to do what he could not (and never would do) in America, and play Othello to Charles Kean's Iago in 1827. Aldridge's Othello was celebrated, and he played the role for the rest of his long career, but his performance remained unique, an oddity, which had very little direct influence on how other actors played the role until Robeson. Aldridge was often controversial just for being a black actor playing a lead Shakespearean role, and his reviewers could be highly insulting about his physical appearance and (in their eyes) racial inferiority. Despite this prejudice, Aldridge established himself as a successful actor in Europe and especially in Russia, where he was enthusiastically received (see Hankey, 2005, pp. 53–56, for a fascinating discussion of his reception in England and Russia). Robeson was different: he was not just a black Othello, an Aldridge for the 20th century. Robeson probably was not even as good an actor as Aldridge. However, he decisively changed the Western approach to the role by playing Othello with a quiet dignity missing from the histrionic Moor familiar to most theatre-goers.

To begin with, Robeson's interpretation of Othello was not well received. Robeson deliberately avoided playing the character as a stereotyped angry, murderous black man. For Robeson, Othello is not simply a man driven mad by jealousy. Othello 'kills not in hate but in honour', Robeson explained, because Desdemona's betrayal represented 'the destruction of himself as a human being, of his human dignity' (Duberman, 1995, p. 274). For some of his fellow actors and directors, this revealed his inexperience. Margaret Webster, who played Emilia and directed Robeson in his famous Broadway productions in the 1940s, was convinced that Robeson was holding something back. She thought he lacked 'the quality of real rage'. Robeson was good at playing Othello's softer lines, Webster thought, particularly when he was with Desdemona whom he romanced with 'tenderness and loving humour'. However, Webster blamed herself for not being able to draw out 'the pent-up emotions' that she expected from the part (Duberman, 1995, p. 271). Uta Hagen, who played Desdemona, worried in rehearsals that 'Robeson is going to be *very* bad' (p. 264). Robeson was not very bad (and Hagen became a staunch defender of Robeson's interpretation): he electrified American audiences, and his production ran in Broadway for more than two years.

The Broadway performance was never filmed. A studio sound recording was made in 1944 and is now easily available on CD. However, it is apparently not reliable as a record of Robeson's performance. According to Lois Potter, it was hastily made, with a reduced cast and without Webster's involvement: 'it is a studio recording', writes Potter, 'and sounds like it' (Potter, 2002, p. 120). Robeson's performance is better captured in live recordings of his subsequent concerts, which often included a recital from *Othello*. Robeson's 1958 concert recording (on the album *Live from Carnegie Hall*) includes a riveting reading of Othello's final soliloquy (5.2.381–99). Unlike the Broadway recording, this was performed before an audience, and so has a vital edge which the studio recording entirely lacks. The speech was Othello's last in the play. Before he began his recitation, Robeson explained to the audience who Othello was. He spoke this introduction with the resounding gravitas of a Baptist preacher (Robeson was the son of a preacher), with a rising and falling cadence that brought a baritone emphasis on unexpected words: 'Othello came from a culture as great as that of ancient Venice, came from an Africa of equal stature, and he felt he was *betrayed*, his honour was *betrayed*, and his *human* dignity was *betrayed*.'

Robeson was using words that he always returned to when discussing the play: dignity, honour, stature, betrayal, human. Each word resonated with the American civil rights movement, in which Robeson himself was a high-profile activist. Webster and many critics at the time seemed to want a different kind of Othello, one in which his monstrous rage could be given a new force by being spoken in the authentic voice of a subjugated black man. However, as the son of a man born into slavery, Robeson needed no method coaching from Webster to make *Othello* a play that belonged to African-Americans.

Following this extraordinary introduction, Robeson briefly explained the scene, and then started the speech with a sudden change of voice, an attack: 'Soft', he said, not softly but with sudden aggression. Then he plunged into a sonorous voice for the next line, before changing tempo again to spit out, with desperate emotion, 'Speak of me as I am!' Then a pause, before 'nothing extenuate' ricocheted from his tongue. The rest of the speech was delivered in the same way, tempos speeding up and then slowing down to an aching pace, his voice soaring one minute, sinking to the bottom of the river the next. And then, with 'Smote him thus' – a sudden interruption, a pause, before he dragged out of the silence, 'No way but this' and then, with a hushed voice, he died 'upon a kiss'.

Robeson's main Shakespearean achievement was to inspire a generation of black American actors for whom Robeson was and remains the definitive Othello. Robeson was not simply a black man playing Othello, he appropriated the role, reinvented it for a generation emerging from social exclusion and looking for a voice that dignified rather than patronised them. Robeson did not so much perform as preach *Othello*. There were many who were directly influenced by watching him. Potter notes a significant rise in the number of black Othellos in America after 1950, among them James Earl Jones, Earle Hyman, Avery Brooks, Joseph Marcell and William Marshall. She also points out that three of these actors (Jones, Brooks and Marcell) have also played Paul Robeson in one-man shows about the singer's life (Potter, 2002, p. 157).

Jones is the most famous and one of the best regarded followers of Robeson. A Hollywood star in his own right (amongst his credits, he was the voice of another jealous black(-suited) lover, Darth Vader), Jones has played Othello seven times, and can make the unusual boast of marrying two of his Desdemonas. He has written a short, valuable book on *Othello* in which he celebrates Robeson's Broadway production as 'the most realised production of *Othello* of modern times'. Robeson gave 'the landmark performance of the 20th century' (Jones, 2003, pp. 98–99). Jones's interpretation of the character is essentially the same as Robeson's: Othello is a warrior, a prince, a vulnerable human being rather than a victim of racial oppression (p. 11). Jones continues: 'Othello does not walk into the world of strangers feeling dependent on their grace; he walks into it expecting them to be dependent on him for wisdom, for knowledge, for experience .... Othello is a superior human being, but not a superman who would exploit others. He possesses grace' (p. 14; Jones quotes his own words from Jones and Niven, 2002, p. 157).

Jones's own performances as Othello have never been recorded. He came close to starring in the BBC's *Othello* in 1981 (see Chapter 5). In 1991, he played himself playing Othello in the film *True Identity*, starring Lenny Henry. Like Robeson, Jones has been captured reciting key speeches from the play. In 2009, Jones read from *Othello* at a Poetry Jam at the White House. The occasion would have intrigued Robeson (who died in 1976), for Jones was speaking to a small audience that included America's first African-American President, Barack Obama, who had just been inaugurated. Robeson would no doubt have played Othello's last speech, as he usually did in his concert performances. The topic was too dark for Jones, who opted instead for Othello's speech to the Venetian Senate (combining 1.3.86–104 with 1.3.142– 83). Robeson was attracted to Shakespeare's portrayal of Othello's nobility in the face of despair; for Jones, the occasion demanded a love story from a man whose life story had enchanted everybody who heard it. Yet both Robeson's and Jones's choices share common themes. They are both statements of identity, of what it means to be a black man in a state dominated by white men (as Robeson might have put it).

Jones's performance (which can be found on youtube.com) echoed Robeson's. He started with 'most potent, grave and reverend Signiors' (l.86), speaking with a Robesonian rolling emphasis, as if feeling the words' strangeness and gravity in his mouth. Jones was more measured and natural in his performance, but his vocal and rhythmic range strongly echoed Robeson. Jones also adapted Robeson's habit of performing against the text to make familiar words sound strange. He was lilting where the verse seems straight-forward, and aggressive in lyrical passages. He spoke "twas strange, 'twas passing strange' with a startled intensity, as if an electric current was running through the words. He varied the tempo unexpectedly, jumping into higher registers and then deepening suddenly into an ebony growl.

The Robeson Othello decisively rewrote and revoiced the charac-ter for a generation of black African-Americans. Robeson achieved this by asserting Othello's dignity, his honour, his grace, and implic-itly linking this interpretation to the American civil rights movement. Through his vocal performance he fought against stereotypes, and rendered the words in the music, rhythms and culture of the 'negro spirituals' (to use Robeson's own words) which he made his career recording. He found unexpected tempos and cadences that fresh-ened the text and made it available for cultural appropriation. In the 2009 White House performance, Robeson's legacy graced the lat-est achievement of the civil rights movement. Jones concluded his performance by looking directly at President Obama, an African-American (and, like Robeson, a lawyer) also celebrated for the power of his voice, and said with a soft growl, 'this only is the witchcraft I have used' (l.183).

'I was to be beautiful. Quite beautiful': Laurence Olivier and John Dexter (1964)

Although controversial, Laurence Olivier's performance as Othello in the 1960s remains one of the touchstones for contemporary per-formances of the play. The long-standing practice of playing Othello as a light-brown skinned Middle Eastern warrior looked out of date against Robeson's authentic African Moor. Olivier decided that, to play Othello, he had to re-ethnicise himself. 'I had to *be* black,' he wrote afterwards, '. . . black down to my soul'. Like Robeson, Olivier did not see Othello as the voice of an oppressed race. On the con-trary, his Othello felt himself to be naturally superior to everybody around him. 'If I peeled my skin, underneath would be another layer of black skin. I was to be beautiful. Quite beautiful' (Olivier, 1987, pp. 98–99).

The production was directed by John Dexter for the National Theatre (of which Olivier was also the artistic director). Olivier was both a critical and commercial success in the role, which was so popular that he had a film made of the production (directed by Stuart Burge in 1965) and he revived the production onstage the following year. Olivier was initially reluctant to take the part on, but his mind was changed by Kenneth Tynan (the National Theatre's Literary Manager), who was determined that Olivier should do it. Olivier was partly reluctant because he did not think the part well written. He imagined that Richard Burbage had boasted to Shakespeare that 'I can play anything you write,' and Shakespeare had written *Othello* to test Burbage's claim. Why was Othello unplayable? 'It's a very badly designed role,' Olivier reflected, 'there are too many climaxes, far too many.' Othello spends most of the play raging, 'bursting eardrums with the throttle full out' (Olivier, 1987, pp. 96–97). Nevertheless, Olivier was flattered when Tynan openly challenged him to take on the role – but was he really responding to Shakespeare's dare to Burbage?

Olivier was also reluctant because he had played Iago in a 1938 production, when he upstaged Ralph Richardson's Othello every night. Olivier did not want to be upstaged himself. Consequently, Olivier played his Othello as if (as he was) desperate to bellow Iago and the other actors off the stage. Olivier took every opportunity to capture the audience's attention: he shouted, he stomped, he cried, he raged, he grabbed, he turned away piteously, he shook his fists at heaven, he buried his head in his hands, he moaned, he whimpered, he snarled. He went through these emotional peaks switching violently from cowed child to murderous savage in the space of a line. Olivier's theatrical excesses made the part very demanding physically, and in the 1965 film, which was shot live, he is visibly panting on the marriage bed at the end just as Lodovico is complaining about the 'tragic loading of this bed' (5.2.407).

From his very first appearance, Olivier's Othello was unsettlingly unpredictable. He entered playing with a rose, which he sniffed coyly, acting more like a teenage lover than a grizzled soldier. In 1.3, when Brabantio accused Othello of bewitching his daughter, Othello looked sour, his lip pushed down in a foul grimace, his body oddly hunched, his hands nervously clutching at the large cross he wore around his neck. However, as soon as the Duke and the Senate made it clear that they would not easily believe that Othello had committed any crime, Othello's demeanour changed completely. He broke out in a broad smile, pushed his shoulders back confidently and engaged his audience with a mesmerising performance of 'Her father loved me . . . ' (1.3.142–84).

Despite his barn-storming theatrics, Olivier came close to being upstaged by Maggie Smith's superb, stoic Desdemona. In her 30s when she took the role, Smith was able to play Desdemona as a more mature woman than is usually played, so adding depth and complexity to the character. Smith's Desdemona was a strong woman, able to control her emotions as Othello raged like a child in front of her. Desdemona never gave in to despair and remained graceful and assertive even in her final scene. She was puzzled and wistful when she dismissed Emilia from her bed chamber, but girlish when talking about his charming 'graces'. She stroked Emilia affectionately when she recalled Barbary, she turned away tearfully on the line 'prithee dispatch', and kept looking at the entrance where Othello last left the stage. She broke into song suddenly, making Emilia stop her work. In the film, Burge introduced one of his very few cinematic devices at this point. As Desdemona sung, he drew the camera back to show Desdemona and Emilia surrounded by a vast stage. They looked unexpectedly vulnerable.

Olivier kept his performance energetic and wildly unpredictable to the very end. In 5.2, he began speaking in a sad voice, clutching Desdemona tenderly to his chest as he asked her if she had 'prayed tonight'. When he told Desdemona that he meant to kill her, she stopped herself from reacting and stayed calm, refusing to rise to Othello's increasingly demented rages. Desdemona's courage was stripped down in stages until she learnt that Cassio was (as Othello believed) dead. Then, finally, she broke down and Othello moved in for the kill. He smothered her with a pillow, then panicked and strangled her. As the scene unfolded, and the truth of Iago's plots emerged, Olivier bellowed louder than ever. He beat his chest, ranted at the heavens, threw himself on Desdemona, and screamed his lines so that they were virtually unintelligible. When Cassio told him about the handkerchief, Othello jumped back on to the bed and started to shake Desdemona as if doing so would revive her. Apart from a few lines of sad reflection, Othello's last words were no less angry. He cut his own throat, still holding Desdemona, and then lowered her, and himself, gently on to the bed to die.

A whole tradition of playing Othello died with him. Although a number of white actors played the role in productions through the 1970s and 1980s, nearly all of these were Olivier-inspired aftershocks. None of them owned the part with the same intensity and commitment as Olivier. For Olivier himself, the part represented something of a summit point for his own Shakespearean career, as he played only one more Shakespearean role onstage after this (Shylock in 1970). With Othello, Olivier was able to legitimately join a long tradition of great Shakespearean tragedians stretching back to Burbage. Olivier's performance was a blockbuster, a 'must-see' piece of event theatre which carried its own legends with it. Even at the time, critics were talking of Olivier's performance as the last major triumph of Romantic theatre. Yet Olivier was also out of his time. Even in 1964, the practice of playing Othello in blackface was beginning to look out of date. Olivier took blackface as far as he could, but not beyond the negative associations which the practice conjures for modern audiences. For Potter his performance, though impressive, was ultimately a hollow impersonation. Even Olivier himself conceded that 'you can never truly do this'.

Othello and politics: Janet Suzman (1987) and Jude Kelly (1997)

Although Robeson used his own success in *Othello* to make a political point, none of his productions were directly pointed at specific topical contexts. Indeed, despite (or maybe because of) the play's clear provocations for modern audiences, productions frequently step back from making direct comment on the situation around them. Two contemporary productions stand out for taking risks with Shakespeare's play to look squarely in the eyes of an audience beset with its own race and gender issues. Janet Suzman directed the play in South Africa when the political debate about white minority rule was at its height; and Jude Kelly directed Patrick Stewart as a white Othello for Washington DC audiences that were unrepresentative of the city's wider racial problems.

The most overtly political *Othello* of modern times is undoubtedly the 1987 production directed by Janet Suzman at the Johannesburg

Market Theatre in South Africa. The production ran for only six weeks on a budget which stretched to an 'Elizabethan' (that is, minimalistic) dressing of an octagonal stage in an old, converted fruit and meat market. Yet the cultural context provided by South Africa, in the dying days of apartheid, made the performance of *Othello* with a black South African (John Kani) playing the lead role a pointedly political gesture aimed at the lingering social prejudices of the white minority class. Suzman and Kani were both activists in the anti-apartheid movement, and both took an enormous personal risk by so openly challenging apartheid orthodoxies, as militant pro-apartheid groups could be violent to those who threatened to destabilise the segregationist policies of the white minority government. Kani had to navigate roadblocks every day to attend rehearsal, and he started the production still mourning the death of his brother at the hands of the police two years earlier. Fortunately, no one involved in the production came to any harm. Apartheid was in its final years, although, as Suzman is at pains to point out in her own, vivid account of the production published ten years later, she did not *know* that the end was nearing. Nelson Mandela was still in jail, and would be for another three years.

Suzman and Kani approached *Othello* as a protest play, a piece of political theatre in which the sexual and the political were intensely entwined. For Suzman, the performance was entirely subsumed in the idea that the marriage and its failure was a metaphor for South Africa in the 1980s. The sexual and political were intimately entwined, she argued, and there could be few acts more political in a racially divided society than an interracial marriage. The play had even more potency if Othello was black, because audiences would be watching a real physical intimacy between a black man and a white woman. Some of the audience walked out in protest at seeing a white woman kissed by a black man, and Suzman received hate mail. Suzman called the often-mooted notion that the marriage is never actually consummated 'piffle' and she thought one of the main advantages of casting a black actor was that he could be more passionate and spontaneous in his affection for Desdemona without fearing that he would smudge the actress' face with make-up (as Olivier famously did). From the beginning, Suzman wanted their relationship to be passionate and physical. 'The story of a mixed marriage,' Suzman wrote, 'systematically destroyed, when you analyse it, on a mere whim, seemed to embrace the larger context of South Africa just perfectly' (Suzman, 1998, p. 24).

Kani's Othello was an innocent man, speaking in a language not his own, in a society to which he was a foreigner. Suzman and Kani took advantage of Kani's own sense of being a stranger in Shakespeare's linguistic world. English was Kani's second language and he had never before performed in any Shakespeare productions. He was working with a white cast and a white director. With only six weeks to rehearse the play, Suzman could afford little time to work on the basics of verse speaking (though she did sacrifice a precious week to focus solely on verse speaking for the whole company). Kani's vocal delivery was remarkable, his natural African accent clipping Shakespeare's verse, making it at turns ordinary and exotic. He spoke like a man unused to speaking in this way, but able to inject into his words a sense of other-worldliness that was both martial and magical. Suzman contrasted Kani with Olivier, whose performance she remembered well. Where Olivier was controlled, she wanted Kani to be innocent and then undone. He was 'a man whose nature would respond to betrayal without self-consciousness'. Of his final lines, addressing Iago as 'that demi-devil', Suzman wrote that it was 'a howl from a soul in torment, a soul that has been gulled by a mind whose machinations are utterly incomprehensible to him. It cannot be considered the cry of a worldly man' (Suzman, 1998, p. 26).

Suzman bravely fashioned Iago as a cipher for Eugene Terre'-Blanche, the founder of the *Afrikaner Weerstandsbeweging* (AWB), a pro-apartheid political movement that promoted the creation of an independent, white Afrikaans state. Terre'Blanche was a particularly controversial figure in the 1980s and was linked to the militant right. For Suzman, the similarity between Iago and Terre'Blanche was too compelling to ignore: they were, she writes, 'both military men, both having a way with words, both possessing an unmistakable streak of vulgarity, both brutal men and racists, both proposing miscegenation as a sin, and both purporting to be trustworthy'. The only difference, she thought, was that Iago was 'subtle' but in all other respects he was the 'spitting image' of the AWB leader (Suzman, 1998, p. 30). In order to explore this interpretation more directly, Suzman deliberately cast Iago against type. She already had an Othello who was much shorter than most actors who play the role. Suzman cast Richard Haines because he was tall, large and bearded, much like

Terre'Blanche. Haines was, says Suzman, 'eager to explore this interpretation'. Iago would be the Terre'Blanche figure eaten up with bitter
disgust at Othello and Desdemona's relationship: he would be the
onstage representative of those who, in the audience, walked out
when Desdemona and Othello kissed, but he would not walk out – he
would stay onstage and destroy the relationship. This created intriguing problems for Suzman, who wanted to avoid Iago's traditional
ability to engage the audience. There was potential to explore white
complicity with apartheid and Terre'Blanche-like figures with the
white audiences that attended the show's first performances, but not
with the black audiences who were queuing up for seats later in the
run. Nor was this a story Suzman wanted to tell. Haines's Iago was
curiously distanced from the audience, he was utterly unsympathetic,
and used his physical bearing to bully as much as entice his victims.
As Hankey puts it, Iago was kept 'public', he was the 'sick face of
Afrikanerdom, of state-sponsored prejudice, rather than a psychotic
individual' (Hankey, 2005, p. 93). Haines's Iago was a nasty, spiteful
man, who spoke deliberately slowly, his words leaden with incipient
violence, his tone capable of viscous sarcasm, but never persuasion or
seduction.

Suzman's *Othello* remains a fascinating example of how a play
like *Othello* can intersect with a dynamic political situation and give
to a society a momentary cultural space in which difficult political
ideas can be tested and explored. But in pitching the play, with all its
theatre history waiting in the wings, into this environment, Suzman
found that the play itself changed. Othello and Desdemona's marriage became more central to the story because of the controversy
that mixing races provoked in South Africa. At the same time, Iago
was a less ambiguous character, his racist agenda was clearer and he
was played so unsympathetically that there was little opportunity for
Iago to seduce the audience.

Jude Kelly's 1997 *Othello* for the Shakespeare Theatre in Washington
D.C. was less successful as a political comment because Kelly and her
star actor Patrick Stewart lacked a direct intimacy with the audience.
Suzman was a part of the history and culture of her own country.
Kelly and Stewart, by contrast, were interlopers to the American civil
rights debate as both are British and White. In an original twist,
Stewart did not black-up; instead, as a gesture to the race politics
that now haunt the play, he and Kelly cast black actors for Iago,

Desdemona and the rest of the Venetian characters. Stewart called this 'photo-negative' casting and the phrase has stuck to the production ever since, even though it is not strictly accurate as Kelly also cast Hispanic actors as Cypriots, and left the colour coding of the play itself unchanged. Stewart was white for the audience, but 'an old black ram' to those onstage. The production seemed to gesture to America's own racial composition, with a white man acting as an empowered minority whose own obsessions gradually turn in on themselves. This is a point that Kelly herself was keen to make: she pointed out that, in Washington, 'approximately sixty percent of the population is black, but it is the thirty percent white minority who hold most of the power and make most of the decisions. And go to the theatre' (*Guardian*, 19 September 1997).

Kelly set *Othello* in a modern, military environment. Othello, Iago and Cassio were professional soldiers, battle-scarred mercenaries, professional guns for hire whose hierarchical allegiances depended upon money and opportunity. Kelly caught the transitory sense of allegiance evident in Roderigo and to an extent in Othello himself, whose migrant identity becomes refigured here from the magical adventurer whose stories seduced Desdemona into a more troubled and restless warrior. Cyprus itself was no island paradise, but a decrepit and bombed out war zone in which identity itself was already fragmented. This was no place for a honeymoon: although sunny, Cyprus was scarred by war and oppression (Potter, 2002, p. 7). Kelly emphasised Othello's mercenary identity by contrasting his military dress with the dress uniforms of the Duke and the Venetians. Iago was played by Ron Canada as a pedantic, note-taking soldier. For some reviewers, the production's major weakness was that the tension between Iago and Othello was diminished by changing the dynamic of their relationship so much. For example, Peter Marks of the *New York Times* complained about 'the disappointingly wan battle of wills between Othello and his nemesis, Iago' (21 November 1997). Canada could never match Stewart's star glamour, he could only brood from the sidelines, trying to direct the gaze of an audience already seduced by Hollywood glitter. As Britons, neither Stewart nor Kelly was in much of a position to comment on Washington's racial problems. In fact, as several reviewers remarked, the production itself side-stepped the race issue altogether, leaving its own questions unanswered.

Othello in small spaces

Modern *Othello*s have relocated the play from main theatres to studio spaces and in doing so have rediscovered *Othello*'s claustrophobic intensity. The publicity that theatres sometimes generate through star casting often overshadows the small scale of the production itself. For example, tickets for Michael Grandage's 2007 Donmar Warehouse production were being traded for hundreds of pounds on the internet by people desperate to see Ewan McGregor play Iago in an auditorium that sat just 250 people. *Othello*'s retreat from the blockbuster stages of Olivier and Robeson into such intimate performance environments was heralded by Trevor Nunn's 1989 production for the RSC. Nunn cast Willard White as Othello, Ian McKellen as Iago and Imogen Stubbs as Desdemona and staged the play in the RSC's tiny studio theatre, The Other Place. Both of these productions explored the impact of *Othello*'s treatment of domestic violence on an audience who are close to the action, entrapped within a relatively small space, unable to escape from Othello's tirades, from Iago's slanders or from the horror of Desdemona's murder.

Nunn made *Othello* a play about interiors, with characters thrown together so closely that they could not help but fall into madness and violence. The stage was dimly lit and mostly bare apart from spartan props such as military camp beds and wooden tables. Lamps were hung from the flies, making the stage feel like a dingy basement room, although for some scenes the stage was bathed in a warm Mediterranean light. Virginia Mason Vaughan sees this sparseness as characteristic of Nunn's naturalistic approach to the play, in which 'evil is not satanic or cataclysmic; it is commonplace, banal, and integral to the texture of everyday life' (Vaughan, 1994, p. 218).

White's performance, like his background, echoed Robeson's. White made his career as a bass baritone and although he was an opera singer, not a pop singer, White has acknowledged his debt to Robeson in an album of his music, *The Paul Robeson Legacy*. Othello is his only notable, non-singing acting role. White played Othello as a greying general who assumed a natural authority in every scene, who spoke with a slow resonant voice, who went at his business with a heavy seriousness.

Desdemona, by contrast, was very young. Stubbs was in her late 20s, but she retained an adolescent freshness which allowed her to play Desdemona as a flighty, coquettish teenager. Desdemona could hardly keep still. She pouted at Othello and teased him, fanned herself dreamily and then skipped about the stage, jumping quickly on Othello's knee. When with him, she spoke like a little girl so that, at times, they seemed almost like father and daughter. Desdemona playfully distracted Othello from his work with hugs and kisses. Asking when Othello would see Cassio, she interrupted his reply with quick questions. Desdemona's 'little girl' act changed suddenly when she kissed Othello, she responded to him lustily, hungrily. Not far beneath these lovers' games was a deep, dark passion. It was hardly surprising then that Othello should be suspicious of Desdemona's childish flirting with Cassio. Cassio was closer to her own age, and, Desdemona teased him, came a-wooing with Othello.

Emilia and Iago looked on with disgust, especially Iago who stood rigid, repulsed. Everything was wrong (to him) about this relationship. Iago was obviously threatened by Desdemona's carefree playfulness. Her movements were an exact contrast to his: where he was upright, precise and well trained, Desdemona was quick, spontaneous. Iago was deeply repulsed by both Desdemona and Othello, and by the thought of them together. McKellen played Iago as a soldier obsessed with order. He stood stiffly, whether on parade or on his own. Getting on to his camp bed, he carefully rolled back the bottom sheets to stop his boots dirtying them, and then got on to the bed with his boots still on. Othello's marriage offended him because it did not fit this precise, physically orderliness at all. In his first soliloquy, McKellen worked hard to shock the audience with his reading of 'I hate the Moor' (1.3.401). He said each word as if possessed by complete hatred, the words not so much spoken as roared, as if it caused him physical pain to say them. This was the only time that the depth of Iago's own madness was exposed. He was, though, a jealous husband himself. McKellen decided to focus on this aspect of the character, and a series of glances between Iago, Emilia and Othello enough to suggest that there might be something to the rumour that Othello and Emilia had been lovers.

Hankey notes that reviewers of this production were unusually interested in the two female leads (Hankey, 2005, p. 99). Zoë Wanamaker played Emilia as a discontented, perhaps bitter wife. The second half of the performance opened with Emilia smoking Iago's pipe and then spotting Desdemona's discarded handkerchief, which had been left onstage, open to the audience, during the interval. She spoke her soliloquy in a weary, almost numbed voice and when Iago entered, addressed him with lines that hovered between threat and innuendo. This was a relationship long grown stale, in which desire had been submerged in contempt. And yet Emilia still made an effort to engage Iago, offering him the handkerchief. Iago held his hand out for it, refusing to get up, expecting Emilia to bring it over. She did so, and then stood behind him, putting her arms around his neck just as Desdemona had done with Othello in the previous scene. This time, though, there was no room for play, Iago just took what he wanted, first easing his pipe out of Emilia's hands, then pulling her to him for a selfish, hungry kiss which nearly suffocated her. He pushed her back abruptly, stared straight ahead, and lit his pipe. Emilia stood stunned for a moment, not sure what to do, nervously rearranged her skirt and then slowly left the stage, without once looking at Iago, who was absorbed in smoking his pipe. The scene dramatised Emilia's later comment about men, said to Desdemona with a long-suffering sense of disillusion: 'Tis not a year or two that shows us a man . . . . They eat us hungrily and when they are full/They belch us' (3.4.113–16).

Nunn exploited Stubbs's and Wanamaker's natural physical similarity by dressing them both in pale cream and white tops. To signify her maturity, Emilia wore a skirt instead of a dress, and she pinned her long blonde hair up where Desdemona let hers down. Emilia was an older, disenchanted version of Desdemona, a glimpse of her future. After undressing Desdemona for bed, Emilia sat back in her chair to reflect cynically on love; Desdemona knelt by her side like a faithful younger sister learning about life's disappointments for the first time. In the final scene, when Emilia hugged the dying Desdemona, her hair was now down, so that the two women seemed to be images of each other. When wounded, after dominating the stage with her accusations against Othello and Iago, Emilia stroked Desdemona's arms and then pulled the sheets over her body, tending her for the last time. She did not die with Desdemona but sat back on a chair by the bed, asserting her role as Desdemona's carer in spite of everything that had been done and said, and then, dead, slumped off the chair onto the stage.

Michael Grandage's 2007 production for the Donmar Warehouse was similarly intense, with audiences trapped with Othello (Chiwetel Ejiofo) and Desdemona (Kelly Reilly) in a small auditorium. The production created dramatic interiors by contrasting darkness with sudden shafts of light breaking from windows above, or from an iron grille over the rear door. Venice was strikingly dank and dismal, with stone floors washed with running water which Iago splashed through in the play's opening scenes. The atmosphere improved little for Cyprus, which was represented by a decaying, crumbling wall and a hot light breaking through the shadows. Thunder rumbled in the background and cicadas clicked restlessly. Cyprus felt like a storm waiting to break. Reviewers immediately noted the production's clammy atmosphere. For Susannah Clapp, the production delivered 'big consequences in a small space' and combined 'intimacy with amplitude' (*Observer*, 9 December 2009); Nicholas de Jongh called it 'misty, crepuscular' (*Evening Standard*, 5 December 2007).

Grandage avoided overdetermining the play with a high-concept period location. Instead of Nunn's Edwardian British Empire setting, Grandage opted for a clear, simple Elizabethan look. The dark stage was filled with simple props such as a table arranged with a bowl of fruit and a pitcher, the bright colours of the fruit brightly lit to make the stage look like a Renaissance still-life painting. The cast wore mainly black Elizabethan costumes so that they almost disappeared when away from the light, especially Othello who, dressed in black, with black skin and beard, was nearly invisible in the dusk. By contrast, Desdemona wore a light cream dress, and her long dark blonde hair, decoratively pinned to her head, shone in the sun. However, in her first appearance, the spotlight that marked her out was too harsh, threatening to burn her for her presumption to determine her own marriage.

Like Nunn, Grandage approached the play as a domestic psychological drama. In rehearsal with the cast, he developed an unusually precise interpretation of Othello and Desdemona's story, which centred on their failure to consummate their marriage. Every time they tried to escape to make love, they were interrupted, and so became increasingly frustrated. Their final scene together was a ruined consummation, with Othello dragging Desdemona off the bed and strangling her in the middle of the stage. For Ejiofor, this scene was an act of love for Othello. He built his interpretation of the role around the idea that Othello 'loved not wisely but too well' (5.2.387). He emphasised Othello's strangeness by speaking with an exotic accent (John Lahr called it an 'African lilt' in his review for *The New Yorker*, 21 January 2008) and moving with a rising and falling walk that one reviewer thought made him look as if he had just come off a boat (Susannah Clapp, *Observer*, 9 December 2007).

Othello was (unusually) noticeably younger than Iago (Ejiofor was 33 at the time) and Reilly played Desdemona as a child-like young bride 'swept up in discovering her own sexual power' (Clapp, 2007). Nicholas de Jongh thought her 'pathetically vulnerable' (*Evening Standard*, 5 December 2007). Desdemona was slender, delicate, with long strawberry blond hair, and she spoke with a reedy, honeyed voice that some reviewers found sexy, others 'over-childish' (Paul Taylor, *Independent*, 5 December 2007). Desdemona's adolescent fragility made her death shocking, especially in the small auditorium of the Donmar Warehouse. De Jongh thought that 'never before has the killing looked as psychopathically brutal'.

Ewan McGregor's Iago was a thin, wiry street thug who lurked in the shadows, staring at Desdemona, Othello and Cassio with razor-sharp eyes. McGregor dropped his natural Scottish accent and instead spoke with clipped vowels, machine-gunning his consonants at Roderigo and Brabantio in the opening scenes. When playing 'honest' Iago, he flashed boyish grins to make himself look sincere to Othello and sinister to the audience. Some reviewers complained that his Iago lacked depth, that his charm was superficial, and that he was too shifty when speaking to the audience. However, McGregor drove the production's pace, rattling through his scenes with a vicious energy that left little time for Roderigo to think or Othello to brood. This pace, combined with Othello and Desdemona's sexual frustration, gave the performance an oppressive urgency. Everything was clearly heading for disaster. McGregor played Iago as an improviser looking to exploit every situation, who threw himself into fast-moving plots with manic energy, surfing the wave of an inevitable tragedy. This breathless pace left the final image of the play as a comment on a ruined world in which a marriage as innocent as Othello and Desdemona's could never flourish. As Michael Billington put it, 'as the spotlight fades on the intertwined bodies of Othello and Desdemona you feel that something of great potential beauty has been destroyed by the world's ugliness' (*Guardian*, 5 December 2007).

Othello on tour

The most intriguing modern *Othellos* have been touring productions which have sought out new audiences for Shakespeare. Between 2008–09, three notable tours of *Othello* used a variety of strategies to attract young audiences and in doing so explored new possibilities for staging the play. Two of these companies, Frantic Assembly and Northern Broadsides, were based in the north of England, with most of their cast speaking in Yorkshire or Lancashire accents which made Shakespeare's verse seem simultaneously unfamiliar and immediate. The RSC *Othello* in 2009 and Frantic Assembly both set the play in a contemporary (or near-contemporary) setting and both used modern theatrical techniques to unsettle audiences from their assumptions about Shakespeare and the play. Northern Broadsides took a more traditional approach by placing *Othello* in a vaguely defined Victorian setting, but director Barrie Rutter found another way to take a risk with the play (and attract new audiences) by casting the comedian Lenny Henry in the lead role.

In 2008, Frantic Assembly toured Britain with a physical theatre adaptation. The company cut the text down to play in a little over an hour, and introduced the production with a long dance sequence which included Othello giving Desdemona the handkerchief. The director, Steven Hoggett, set the play in a modern, dingy northern pub with a pool table in the centre, surrounded by bottles and used cigarettes, and flanked by a persistently flashing fruit machine. Jimmy Akingbola played Othello as a bouncer fighting to be top dog in a viscously racist, working-class gang. Claire-Louise Cordwell played Desdemona as a young tomboy who thought nothing of draping herself over the men onstage. The women (among them Bianca, promoted to be one of the main characters) wore tight track-suits emblazoned with jewelled letters, gossiped in the lavatory and swapped fags. In the pub, they were treated roughly by the men, who pushed them up against the wall or down on to the table. Othello and Desdemona's affair had no chance in this world of easy violence. Fights broke out regularly, with disputes settled with pool sticks and broken bottles. As Lyn Gardner put it, 'there is a terrible animal beauty in their coiled violence and vulgarity, a diseased nobility like lions in a zoo suffering from mange and misdirected aggression' (*Guardian*, 29 September 2008). The set walls concertinaed to show Othello's delirium as he murdered Desdemona on the pool table. Othello stumbled against the walls, which folded in and out. As realistic as the setting was, the environment was itself implicated in the disaster, as if the aftershocks of Othello's crime were rippling through reality itself.

Like Willard White (and Paul Robeson), Lenny Henry had never played Shakespeare before he starred in Barrie Rutter's 2009 touring production for Northern Broadsides. The closest he had come was when he tried to break Hollywood with the film *True Identity* (1991), in which he played a black man who encounters James Earl Jones playing Othello. Henry made his career in light entertainment (and once worked with *The Black and White Minstrel Show*), so his casting was risky, but the production became a critical and commercial success. Henry's Othello was a large man who looked uncomfortable in the blood-red military uniforms worn by the cast. He spoke with a deep bass voice that sounded like aged leather as Othello descended into jealous madness. Although Henry avoided Olivier's excesses, he was much less restrained than Ejiofer. Rutter made much of Henry's physical height and strength. Othello was able to pick up Jessica Harris's Desdemona with one arm. As his jealousy deepened, he became more and more agitated, his voice growled, raged, rose to a self-pitying pitch, descended into murderous certainty, often in the same speech. In his final scenes, he discarded his uniform, so that he wore only a white sleeveless vest on his upper body, exposing his broad, muscular arms. He leaned over Desdemona like an uncaged animal finding its prey, his arms either side of her, almost as big as she was. It seemed inevitable that this Othello would overwhelm Desdemona.

In 2009, Kathryn Hunter directed a touring production for the RSC with Patrice Naiambana as Othello and Natalia Tena as a socially awkward Desdemona. Hunter set the play in the 1950s to make it more relevant to a contemporary audience. Hunter told Mark Lawson that 'the aim of the production is to make as visceral as possible the destruction of someone hated for their otherness' (*Guardian*, 27 January 2009). They also became very interested in the role of the military in constructing notions of honour and of behaviour. Hunter took the cast to Sandhurst Military Academy for lessons on how to be a soldier, and even invited one of the officers to attend rehearsals to drill the cast. Michael Gould's small-minded Iago exploited the situation because he enjoyed destroying people. He had already nearly ruined Emilia, who was played by Tamzin Griffin as an embittered alcoholic. The cast were keenly aware of the contemporary context of race and together watched the inauguration of President Barack Obama during rehearsals. (As part of the educational activities which supported the production, the RSC ran a workshop with the curious premise *Is Obama the new Othello?*) The military hierarchy was a clear structure for the cast to build their performance on. Othello was respected for his military abilities, but loathed when he took a white woman as his bride. In a clever reimagining of 2.2, Hunter showed a singer blacking up for a show and playing lewdly with a golliwog doll to demonstrate his contempt for Othello's marriage. As Lyn Gardner put it in her review for the *Guardian*, 'no wonder Othello goes mad; he is already living a double life in which his standing as a general and standing as a man are quite at odds with each other' (Guardian, 7 February 2009).

Conclusion

Othello is far from being the least performed of Shakespeare's plays, but the problem of finding an appropriate cast for the play has meant that there are fewer mainstage productions than there used to be. Those actors for whom playing Iago or Othello is a career ambition have tended to do so in small-scale theatres. In turn, *Othello* itself has become a different kind of play. The terrifying, extravagant rages of Olivier, even the sonorous, epic reading of Robeson, belong to a time when productions of *Othello* were as much about the actor as the play. On the modern stage, another *Othello* has emerged in the more intimate studio theatres in which it now often plays. This *Othello* is a domestic, psychological thriller rather than a boisterous melodrama. The play is also more of an ensemble work, with Emilia in particular emerging as one of the play's most affecting parts.

The play's end is still shocking, even more so because the audience can interact with Othello in a way not possible in a large proscenium arch theatre. The scene's violence is terrifying when close at hand as the audience are drawn into Othello's conviction that he commits no murder, but performs a sacrifice. In 2007, Eamonn Walker discovered how Othello could usurp Iago and use the audience in a production at the reconstructed Globe Theatre in London (directed by Wilson Milam). Walker's performance is captured in a well-made live film of the production which, unusually for such films, does an excellent job of capturing the relationship between actor and audience. In his final scene, Walker literally commanded the stage. His opening speech, so often delivered as an internal monologue, was instead addressed to the audience, as if Othello felt he had to justify himself. The bed was placed centre stage, with the sleeping Desdemona positioned so that her feet faced the stage doors, her head to the audience standing in the pit.

Othello entered the stage with attendants and then stood solemnly right in front of the doors, a sword in his arm held with the handle lying across his chest, waiting for the attendants to leave. When they did so, he turned suddenly, locking the door. No one was going to disturb him. He, Desdemona and the audience were locked in together. He then turned back, paused for a moment, and walked slowly towards the bed, his sword still held by the blade, as if for a ceremony. He spoke the first line, 'it is the cause' (5.2.1), standing at the foot of the bed, facing the audience. He was dressed in white, he held his sword like a sceptre, and he spoke as if he were a priest about to offer a sacrifice. The next time he said, 'it is the cause', he rolled his eyes upwards, as if to heaven, and he started to breath hard as if approaching some sort of religious ecstasy, his next words, 'let her not shed her blood' spoken like a prayer. Then, insisting firmly that 'she must die', Othello walked round the bed to the front of the stage. He did not carry a light, so when he said 'put out the light', he implied that the light was somewhere in the audience by addressing the audience. When he repeated the line, he pointed to Desdemona behind him without looking at her and still staring at the audience, as if to say: this is what needs to happen, this is what we need to do, there is no choice. From this point, Othello's focus turned away from the audience to Desdemona herself, who Othello prowled around as if he were a lion scenting its prey, his hands cupped as if in prayer. As he continued, he kept extending his arm over Desdemona, his hand ready to grab her, and then recoiling, almost as if he were pulling bunches of invisible strings from her, drawing the betrayal out of her.

Walker continued to explore this interpretation when Othello finally killed Desdemona. The scene was noisy and messy. Desdemona resisted until the end and both her lines and Othello's were shouted so much they could hardly be understood. Language fell into inarticulate screams, Othello crying as much as Desdemona. She first tried to escape, struggling at the locked door. Othello walked over to her, picked her up and carried her over his head, again like a priest at a sacrifice, and dropped her on to the bed. As she scrambled away, Othello knelt over her, pulled her head back in his arms and smothered her with his forearm, howling as she struggled. The audiences were not just witnesses, as the intimacy of the stage meant that they were also complicit in Othello's madness. Why did no one get up on the stage *and stop him?*

5   The Play on Screen

Othello was first filmed in 1906 and a number of short silent movies followed. The play's vivid stage pictures suited the monochrome, voiceless melodrama of the early years of the cinema. Since then, *Othello* has continued to attract film-makers, actors and writers with the consequence that there exist more than 20 versions in a variety of languages. However, cinema and television faced similar challenges to the theatre as the cultural politics of representing race and sexual violence shifted. In 1981, director Jonathan Miller was accused of being racist for casting the white actor Anthony Hopkins in the title role. Cinema and television have been more ready to dispense with Shakespeare's text than the theatre, and since those first silent movies the play's text has been rewritten, sometimes drastically so. Most films cut the text so that it better fits the expectations of modern audiences. Some films have dispensed with the text altogether, retaining the play's structure and characters but writing new dialogue that puts the play into an immediate, contemporary context. In this chapter, I shall discuss in more detail the most widely available examples of each of these approaches. I shall begin with a discussion of the best-known films of the text as written (even if heavily cut), then go on to talk about two significant modern-day adaptations.

Othello as *Film Noir*: Orson Welles (1952)

Orson Welles's striking 1952 film had a troubled history. Welles raised funds by literally prostrating himself in front of potential backers and taking well-paid parts in popular Hollywood movies to keep the production afloat (Estrin, 2002, p. 33). Consequently, the film was shot haphazardly over a number of different countries as budget, time and location presented Welles with opportunities to continue with filming. A shot of a punch being thrown was filmed in one country and the shot of Iago taking the punch was filmed months later in another country. When finally finished, the film was a critical success in Europe, where it won the Palme d'Or at the Cannes Film Festvial. *Othello* was barely noticed in America, and was hardly seen until its restoration in the 1990s. Because of this patchwork of filming and restoration, the film now available is a curate's egg. *Othello* is visually impressive, but as a performance of the play it is surprisingly old-fashioned. The film looks like a European, expressionist work, but the actors were dressed as if they were understudies for a 1950s doublet-and-hose production.

Welles was determined not to play *Othello* as a domestic psychodrama and did everything he could to stop audiences feeling as if they had access to its characters' emotional lives. Close-ups (usually a mainstay of Shakespearean films) were used very sparingly. Instead, Welles dwelt on surfaces, finding external ways to signify the play's tragic themes. Much of the film was composed of long-shots, which typically located a character shadowed against an imposing backdrop such as a raging sea, a towering castle wall or a bleak sky. These characters were fragile, small people in an indifferent universe, dominated by structures and forces with little interest in their stories. Actors rarely looked directly into the camera, or even into each other's eyes. When forced to bring characters into closer view, Welles deliberately filmed them from disorientating angles.

To avoid intimacy with the characters, Welles used images to suggest action, and told his story through objects rather than people. Iago lived in a world shaped by cages. He began the film in a cage suspended over the castle wall, looking contained but not destroyed as, below him, the bodies of Desdemona and then Othello were led out on biers, followed by monks who appear in a stark silhouette against the sky. By starting the film with the play's end, Welles established that this would be Iago's story: he sees the end, and through his eyes the film traces the events that led up to Othello's death and Iago's imprisonment. There were cages all through the film, foreshadowing Iago's fate. The cage itself was in one scene, swinging emptily as if waiting for Iago to occupy it; the shadows of windows fell across Iago and Othello like the bars of a cell; and, most strikingly, the wooden slats of a soldier's sauna became a prison for both Iago and Roderigo. Robert Coote played Roderigo as a slightly unhinged dandy easily led by Iago. He carried a poodle everywhere with him, and after stabbing

Cassio in the sauna scampered through steamy corridors after his dog, only to be trapped by Iago above. In a series of frenzied, disjointed shots of Iago's sword flashing like jagged lightning through slats in the ceiling, Iago stabbed Roderigo to death from the floor above.

Othello (played by Welles) was dark and impenetrable. When Othello 'put out the light' (5.2.7), his own face came close to vanishing: only his eyes, his teeth and vague hints of blackened skin were visible. One shot began with complete darkness, then Othello's face appeared in the lower right hand corner of the screen, looking petty against the overwhelming blackness. When he raged against Desdemona, his face filled the screen in such a way that it was impossible to see where his face ended and the darkness began. Othello's face, dissolving into the background, seemed to become like the indifferent landscapes which dominated the film and those in it: it was as if Othello was now an elemental force, not an animal as in some versions of the play, but something beyond human, beyond morality. Desdemona stood out against the background because she wore a white dress which seemed to glow in the candlelight. She was as still as Othello, who killed her with a semi-transparent scarf. Welles's stylised presentation limited the scene's traumatic impact, turning Desdemona's death into a bleak, slow sacrifice.

The film is a curiosity with performances which do not live up to Welles's cinematic ambitions. Even in the restored version the sound quality remains poor, dialogue is hard to hear, and the stylistic distancing devices make it hard to fully engage with the characters and their story. Yet the film is utterly unique in *Othello*'s history. By stepping away from the characters, the film negated the play's exploration of race and sexual violence (for which it has been criticised, see Vaughan, 1994, p. 199). Instead, Welles created a brooding, philosophical *Othello* that focused on tragic destiny rather than identity politics.

'Who hast done this deed?': Jonathan Miller (1981)

In the BBC's 1981 *Othello*, Anthony Hopkins became the last major actor to wear blackface for the title role. Directed by Jonathan Miller, *Othello* was originally broadcast in the fourth season of the BBC's ambitious *Complete Works* series and is now widely available on DVD. The BBC had recently attracted criticism for casting a white actor to play an Indian in the popular sitcom *It Ain't Half Hot Mum* (which itself ended in 1981) and faced a backlash against *Othello* as well. Many critics at the time (and since) went as far as to accuse Miller of being racist (Potter, 2002, p. 154). Ironically, the BBC had originally wanted James Earl Jones to play Othello, but the actors' union Equity protested that there were British black actors better able to take on the role. When Miller took over the production, he petulantly sidestepped the issue by casting Hopkins, a white actor, instead (Willis, 1991, p. 121). Jones later said he had no regrets about not being part of the production, which he thought was an 'unfulfilled' *Othello* in which Hopkins 'seemed lost' (Jones, 2003, p. 109).

If Jones would have given the BBC an Othello in the Robeson mould, Hopkins brought with him an iteration of the character that was indebted to Olivier. Hopkins had a detailed knowledge of Olivier's work having been at the National Theatre when Olivier played the part in his 1966 revival. Hopkins brought to the role an extraordinary range of physical gesture which enabled him to trace Othello's fall from a powerful general to an animal-like raving monster. Hopkins's Othello was a Middle Eastern soldier, with lightly browned skin. Almost as if to distract from his face, Hopkins's hair was shaggy, untameable and practically standing on end in the Venetian scenes, when Othello looked swarthy and virile next to the white-haired old men of the Senate. On arrival in Cyprus, Othello was commanding and jubilant, entering dressed in armour, his arms outstretched victoriously. In the film's early scenes, Othello was preoccupied with impressing those around him with his ability to dominate social situations. He was a natural self-dramatiser who could ably enchant the Venetian Senators with his account of wooing Desdemona (played by Penelope Wilton). Even his lines to Desdemona seemed to be said for show. But the same characteristics which made him seem so potent here also made him look wild in his later scenes. As Iago played on Othello's doubts, Hopkins drew himself physically inwards. His Othello now obsessively analysed everything, he avoided making eye contact, he frequently appeared hunched and withdrawn. He looked like an animal. Before his fit, Othello brooded wolf-like about Desdemona, then lurched backwards suddenly, growling and frothing at the mouth.

He was watched by Iago, played by Bob Hoskins as a snarling 'inhuman dog' who had finally brought down his master. If Jones had taken the role, he may not have been as 'lost' as he thinks Hopkins was, but he would have been frustrated by Iago, who Jones thought 'lacking' and 'without grace' (Jones, 2003, p. 109). This was no accident: Hoskins was deliberately cast to be a graceless, working man's soldier with a crude sense of humour (Willis, 1991, p. 121). Hoskins had established a reputation for playing cockney gangsters in films such as *The Long Good Friday* (1980) and Miller wanted to give Iago a similar kind of brutish indifference to suffering. Potter calls him 'cheerfully psychotic' because he was constantly laughing to himself, delighted at his ability to manipulate others. The film ends with Hoskins's off-screen laughter 'ringing down the now-empty corridors' (Potter, 2002, p. 154). Willis calls him 'impish', 'troublemaking' and 'destructive' with a bent for rude, bestial gestures (Willis, 1991, p. 122).

The final unravelling of Othello's character began with a clever shot in which Othello stood in the shadows at the entrance to his bedroom. To one side of him, inside the room, a large mirror reflecting Desdemona's near-dead body at the back of the room, although Desdemona herself was out of shot. When Emilia (played by Rosemary Leach) discovered her, the camera did not move but stayed fixed on the mirror. With nothing visual dominating the shot, Miller left it to Emilia's voice to focus the scene. Emilia sobbed over Desdemona's body, and Desdemona's lines were spoken so softly they were virtually inaudible. Othello meanwhile stood awkwardly, in the middle of buckling his sword belt. When Emilia called 'Help' (5.2.140) he momentarily put his arms forward, his hands upturned, as if he actually *could* help. But this was a momentary lapse, his hands fell again, and he stood utterly still. Miller allowed the camera to capture the experience of all three characters, and to see what Othello sees, but did so in a way which distanced the viewer from all of them, as if the tragedy was either too personal or too immense to capture in an image. Instead, he allowed Othello to look pathetic. Othello did not know what to do or how to respond. He did not even react when Emilia exclaimed, 'Who hast done this deed?' (5.2.143). The camera betrayed Othello's guilt; so did his inaction, his hesitation at the threshold of his bedroom, which he seemed momentarily unable to cross. Miller kept the camera completely still for nearly two minutes on this shot, with Emilia speaking only three lines, and Desdemona's faint voice dying into a 30-second silence. Othello seemed broken already.

These were the most compelling aspects of an otherwise over-cooked film. Potter also praises Wilton's and Leach's performances (Potter, 2002, p. 155), and Lynda E. Boose has written an excellent essay on Miller's use of television as a form; yet both also draw attention to the film's faults, and Boose feels compelled to acknowledge, from the start, that the film is 'not an ideal production' (Boose, 1997, p. 186). Miller created an intricate and rich visual world heavily influenced by Renaissance painters such as Johannes Vermeer and Georges de la Tour. The production's sensuously painted interiors made the drama seem very intimate, but by the end of the film that intimacy had become stifling. Miller hardly cut the text at all and ran scenes at a crushingly slow pace, with many lines soft-spoken direct to camera. What should have been a gripping, tense drama was rendered into a stately, incremental study of madness.

A Sex Tragedy: Oliver Parker (1995)

Oliver Parker's 1995 movie remains the most lavish and highest profile film of *Othello* available. The film was born out of a brief renaissance in Shakespeare film-making which began with Kenneth Branagh's sun-drenched *Much Ado About Nothing* (1993) and reached its high-water mark with Baz Luhrmann's *William Shakespeare's Romeo+Juliet* (1997). Like Luhrman and Branagh, Parker cast star actors in the lead roles and tightened the script to make it better fit the fast-paced rhythms of modern cinema, bringing out the play's sensuous and sexual themes. All of this was designed to bring audiences, particularly young audiences, to Shakespeare. Parker had both star power and theatrical ability in his Othello: Laurence Fishburne's Hollywood reputation for playing hard-edged, street characters was already well established, but Fishburne was also a respected off-Broadway actor acclaimed for his work with the African-American playwright August Wilson. The film's other star was Kenneth Branagh, who played against type by taking the villain's part.

Parker approached *Othello* as a sex tragedy. In the first shot of the film, nocturnal lovers drifted past on gondolas. As one boat drew close, the camera momentarily revealed the occupants to be a black man and a white woman in each other's arms. We soon learnt that they were not Othello and Desdemona, but before we saw the man's face he put up a white tragic mask to hide himself, as if aware of the camera watching him. The mask's frozen downturned face seemed incongruous for a romantic setting. The black lover was hidden by the white tragedian, almost as if Parker wanted to acknowledge, and perhaps mock, the past practice of using blackface. The shot also foreshadowed the tragedy implied by illicit sexuality. Another boat passed, this time a woman's hand pulled a curtain across. Everyone on the river had something to hide.

The film's several sex scenes added some contemporary spice to the play, but also developed the idea that love is something that needs to be hidden, veiled. The play has no sex scenes, but the film has several: Othello and Desdemona together, Cassio and Desdemona (as Othello imagined it), Cassio and Bianca, and even Iago and Emilia. In each case, the bed dominated the scene: Othello and Desdemona stood by a bed, Iago wrestled with Emilia on one. As Cyprus celebrated its victory outside, Othello and Desdemona faced each other, Othello half naked. Parker took care to emphasise distance between them. Although not explicitly stated, this seemed to be their first sexual encounter and both seemed afraid of physical intimacy, Desdemona even stepping back slightly as Othello unbuttoned his trouser belt. The camera then played coy itself, retreating to the ceiling (the shot resembled the perspective, but not the quality, of a CCTV camera) to voyeuristically watch as Desdemona removed her dress in front of Othello and then, quickly, jumped into the veiled bed, her nakedness only momentarily visible. She then pulled Othello through the muslin curtains that surrounded the bed and the camera followed them as they made love, focusing in on their arms, thighs, face but never revealing their whole bodies.

Later, Parker explained Othello's jealousies through a dream sequence in which Othello imagines Cassio making love to Desdemona in his bed. Parker set up Othello's fall by showing Iago and Othello sparring outside, watched by Desdemona. Othello beat Iago easily, evidently conscious that he was being watched by Desdemona. He looked up to her standing on a balcony overlooking the practice area, and shouted up to her 'Excellent wretch!' In the following scenes, as Iago worked his 'poison', Othello was haunted by dreams of Cassio and Desdemona together, their hands clenched on a white sheet strewn with red petals to look just like the spotted handkerchief (a motif which Parker returned to later when Othello, Cassio and Iago all had spots of blood on their white tunics). Othello killed Desdemona whilst lying by her on the bed. Parker found an unexpected tenderness, a sense of care, in the way Othello smothered her. As she struggled, Parker stayed focused on Othello: he was crying. Desdemona's hand crept up to feel Othello's tears, clutching at his nose and mouth, almost as if she wanted to suffocate him. But as she weakened, her hand started to caress his face, and then went limp. Parker decided to cut Desdemona's last words; instead, when Emilia found her, she died immediately. Last words were not necessary: Parker had shown all he needed to with these last shots. After stabbing himself, Othello dragged himself on top of Desdemona for his dying kiss, so that both were together again in bed. The film's final shot directly echoed the film's beginning by showing a boat at sea. The bodies of Othello and Desdemona were wrapped together in white cloth and tipped into the water, the camera following them before the screen faded to the credits.

Parker added a further sex scene between Iago and Emilia to contrast Othello's love-making – sensuous, considerate, coy, exotic – with Iago's brutish, selfish sexuality. Emilia taunted Iago with the handkerchief on their bed. Iago jumped on her, violently turned her round so she faced the bed, and, as he pushed her dress up ready to rape her, he snatched the handkerchief away. The camera closed in on Iago, obliterating Emilia completely from view, for his brief, triumphant aside to camera. Then Iago tossed the handkerchief into the air and lunged out of shot towards Emilia. The camera stayed with the handkerchief, which seemed to flutter into darkness. Iago seemed to be incapable of the kind of love that Othello experienced. Sex was for him about self-pleasure and domination. Parker ended Iago's story with a curious innovation that hinted that Iago secretly envied the heightened passion which Othello and Desdemona achieved in their marriage. Abandoned by Cassio, Iago pulled himself on to the bed to lie at Othello and Desdemona's feet. Emilia was also dead on the bed, beside Desdemona. The camera pulled back for a last shot of the main characters, lifeless, their blood reddening the sheets.

Adapting *Othello*

As well as being frequently filmed, *Othello* has been used as an underlying template for several modern films. These act like cinematic
translations, taking the structure of the play and remixing its key
relationships to create a new, modern work. A situation is usually
established – a police force, a high school, even a jazz club – which
forms a backdrop in which the story of a man ruining a mixed-race
marriage can be played out.

In 1963, Basil Dearden directed *All Night Long* with Patrick
McGoohan as Johnny Cousin (Iago), Paul Harris as Aurelius Rex
(Othello) and Marti Stevens as Delia Lane (Desdemona). The film was
set in a London jazz club in the early 1960s and included several
major jazz artists (David Brubeck, Charlie Mingus) playing themselves. Dearden introduced a few twists to Shakespeare's story so, for
example, the handkerchief became a cigarette case. Delia was a sassy
jazz singer who had given up her career to marry Rex. Johnny Cousin
wanted to put his own band together with Delia, who he was also
in love with. When Delia coolly refused him, and told him never to
speak to her again about love, Johnny resolved to destroy her marriage. The film riffed on *Othello*, taking its main themes and alluding
slyly to aspects of the play without speaking Shakespeare's text.

This was a strategy copied by Andrew Davies who, in 2001,
wrote an updated version of *Othello* for television. His Othello was
John Othello (Eamonn Walker), London's first black police commis-
sioner, who was married to Dessie Brabant (Keeley Hawes). Othello
was driven to murder by one of his staff, Ben Jago (Christopher
Eccleston). Other elements were updated too. Rather than a handkerchief, Othello's 'ocular proof' was a silk dressing gown which (revers-
ing Shakespeare's version) Desdemona gave to Othello and which
featured prominently in sex scenes. When Othello found Michael
Cass (Richard Coyle) wearing the dressing gown, he concluded that
Cass too had been making love to Dessie.

Like Dearden, Davies strengthened Jago's motives. At the start
of the film Jago was Othello's superior, but in an effort to look
progressive, the police promoted Othello over Jago. From the beginning, then, Jago was angry to be passed over by his own protégé.
Davis made much of their tortured relationship by making sure that
Jago's racism was tinged with homoeroticism. Davies retained Iago's

direct addresses to the audience so that the view of the play and of its characters was firmly located in Jago's warped perspective. Early in the film, Othello told Jago about his promotion. Although clearly stunned, Jago masked his anger with a suddenly ebullient show of masculine affection, grabbing Othello and calling him 'you clever big black bastard'. As they hugged, the camera swung round to reveal Jago's broad smile turning sour and angry. Jago hid his racism behind such thin masculine bravado. The next shots cleverly translated the Shakespearean soliloquy into a modern idiom, as Jago stormed through the police station firing spiteful one-liners at the camera, mocking Othello's race (at one point waving his hands like a blackface minstrel). Each line was shot in a different part of the station, with the speech cut together in a fast-paced, disorientating way to convey Jago's state of mind.

Eccleston's Jago was a much more fragile, unstable character than Shakespeare's Iago and was noticeably less confident than his wife Estelle (Emilia). Iago's question, 'Did Michael Cassio, when you wooed my lady, / Know of your love' (3.3.105–06) was rephrased as, 'Mike Cass is spending more time with 'er than you at the moment. You all right about that then?' Jago also made Othello doubt Dessie's faithfulness by saying, 'Well, Dessie, you can tell she's put her wild times behind her'. Eccleston created a strange, boyish, manic Jago, capable of bizarre behaviour, blunt northern innuendo and abrupt mood changes. For many reviewers, Ecclestone's performance stole the show, perhaps at the expense of the other actors (see Lisa Hopkins's (2002) review for *Early Modern Literary Studies*).

Othello was also modernised that same year in a major Hollywood film, *O*. Like Davies's film, *O* is a contemporary version of the *Othello* story with the characters, language and situation updated to tell the story of the only black teenager in a white school's basketball team. Odin (the film's Othello, Mekhi Phifer) was quickly promoted as the team's star player, and fell in love with the school's most popular girl, Desi (Julia Stiles). His jealous nemesis was Hugo (Josh Hartnett). Odin's madness was explained as a retreat into cocaine addiction. Othello kills Desdemona after taking cocaine in the film's bleak finale. He started to make love to her, but then put his hands around her neck to choke her. Here, the film echoed Shakespeare as he repeated to himself the words 'I wish I could but I can't, I can't.' Unlike Davies's film, *O* made Desdemona a strong woman unafraid to speak her mind. When Odin confronted her about the scarf, she retorted, with teen attitude, 'What?! If you want to ask me if I'm cheating on you go ahead and get some balls and ask!' The language and emotional register captured the outspoken personal dramas of reality talk shows such as *The Jerry Springer Show*: it was hard-edged, emotive, wise-cracking and diffident.

In updating *Othello* for contemporary audiences, all three films adopted remarkably similar strategies. None of them depended on audiences knowing *Othello* (only Davies's production uses the name Othello for the title and main character), but neither did they stray too far from the outline story. Characters were given new names that sounded like modern versions of their Shakespearean counterparts. All three put *Othello* into a modern setting, and all were careful to establish a strong context with a defined hierarchy to bring out the Iago character's bitterness at being passed over. Iago's motivations were clarified, each film assuming that modern audiences prefer motives which can be simply and consistently defined. Desdemona was a strong, independent woman in all of these films, and in each one Othello was played by a black actor. Although little remained of Shakespeare's texts in any of the adaptations, all retained the narrative structure and character dynamics which Shakespeare crafted, and all kept the vivid, shocking images with which the play concludes.

Conclusion

Othello may have declined in the theatre, but its cinematic life is a healthy one. The success of *Othello* on the silver screen says much about the degree to which the play's striking visual images can be translated into a medium where the visual is always more important than the verbal. *Othello* is a very visual play, even though sight turns out to be untrustworthy. Cinema gives us 'ocular proof' that *Othello* can continue to have a powerful impact on contemporary imaginations.

6 Critical Assessment

Othello is one of Shakespeare's most discussed plays, and has been a source of critical fascination since the 17th century. The number of publications about *Othello* has accelerated in the last 20 years, and anyone now confronted with the range and depth of this material will find it utterly daunting. *Othello* is not a play that is easily reducible to key themes and tragic flaws. Shakespeare told the story in a way which seems to defy narrative logic. Iago either has no motive, or he has several; Othello may or may not be royal; the handkerchief may be a magical heirloom, a token of fidelity – or just a spotted handkerchief. Time and location shift in different ways. The only character we get to know, through revealing soliloquy, is Iago, and we never really get to know him: 'I am not what I am,' he insists. Iago constructs the story for us, mediates our understanding of it, and yet no character in Shakespeare is a more untrustworthy guide, and at the point when he most needs to speak, when he is compelled to explain himself, he retreats into permanent silence. *Othello* cannot be contained within critical discourse, which often seems to flounder in attempts to describe the play's horrors. This is a play in which the central character literally has a fit, who reveals his monstrosity, and yet never loses his dignity, even bestowing on the murder of his lover the aura of a duty, a rite. *Othello* is a baffling play whose effects disturb at levels which resist critical analysis, with a madness which runs ahead of any attempt to contain and contextualise. As Samuel Johnson once observed, the play 'can draw no aid from critical illustration' (Vickers, 1974, p. 165).

Nevertheless, certain questions have long haunted writers trying to find a critical language to describe *Othello*'s strange, unsettling tragedy. One is about Othello himself: who is Othello, how do we account for his fall and what is the relevance of his race and skin colour? The other is about Desdemona: what is the nature of her love for Othello, why does it offend so many people in the play and how aware is she of the power that her private desires have on the society around her? These highly contested areas have dominated discussion of *Othello* almost from the beginning, and sometimes crowd out other critical possibilities (of which there are many). In the early modern period, and even later, the questions were posed with prejudices against Africans and women typical of their time. In recent years, the same questions have been reformulated with a new urgency, as Shakespeare's treatment of race and gender has been thoroughly reconsidered in the light of contemporary interest in those issues. They are not the only questions to ask of the play, but they are highly relevant to the play's performance, not least because critics frequently turn to the theatre, and to the play's casting debates, to explore how *Othello*'s interpretative history has been shaped by, and in turn itself influenced, evolving cultural attitudes to race, gender and sexuality. In this survey, I shall focus on these questions, first considering how early critics of the play posed them and then turning to contemporary approaches to race and gender.

The tragedy of the handkerchief

Othello's first critic was severe. Thomas Rymer, writing at the end of the 17th century, scorned the play's artifice and absurd plot devices in a long polemical attack which remains one of the wittiest broadsides against Shakespeare. Rymer scoffs at the title 'Moor of Venice' which, he writes, is a 'Note of pre-eminence, which neither History nor heraldry can allow him', going on to write that 'it is an affront to all Chroniclers and Antiquaries, to top upon 'um a Moor'. Rymer quotes a line from Horace to prove his point: 'Sed non ut placidis coeant immitia, non ut serpentes avibus geminentur, tigribus agni', or in other words, 'but not so far that savage should mate with tame, or serpents couple with birds, lambs with tigers' (Vickers, 1974, p. 27). Rymer is particularly incredulous that Desdemona should marry a 'Black-amoor': 'with us a *Moor* might marry some little drab, or Small-coal Wench: *Shakespeare* would provide him the Daughter and Heir of some great Lord or Privy-Councellor, and all the Towne should reckon it a very suitable match' (p. 29). This is the beginning, but not the end, of Rymer's withering attack on the play, every element of which he dissects. He calls Desdemona a fool, mocks the 'verse rumbling in our ears' (p. 30), calls Iago and Desdemona's dialogue in 2.1, 'a long rabble of Jack-pudden farce' (p. 37) and laughs at the use of the handkerchief as a plot device: 'so much ado, so much stress, so much passion and repetition about an Handkerchief! Why was not this call'd the *Tragedy of the Handkerchief*? What can be more absurd . . . ?' (p. 51).

Rymer's views were not shared by everyone, and in 1694 Charles Giddon wrote a spirited and enlightened response. Giddon broke Rymer's criticism down to essentially two charges: that a Moor would never be privileged by the State, and that a white woman of Desdemona's rank would never marry a Moor. To the first, Giddon concedes that 'a *Negro* here does seldom rise above a Trumpeter' but ascribes this to 'the Vice of Mankind, which is the Poet's Duty . . . to correct, and to represent things as they should be, not as they are'. He goes on to write, 'there is no reason in the nature of things why a *Negro* of equal Birth and Merit should not be on an equal bottom with a *German, Hollander, French-man,* &c' (Vickers, 1974, p. 73). Turning to the question of miscegenation, Giddon takes Rymer to task for his use of Horace: 'unless he can prove that the Colour of a Man alters his Species and turns him into a *Beast* or *Devil* 'tis such a vulgar Error . . . to allow nothing of Humanity to any but our own Acquaintance of the fairer hew'. Othello, he reminds us, is both a Christian and of royal blood so, if anything, it is Desdemona who is 'advanc'd' by the match (p. 74). He concludes this point by noting many such relationships in the Indies and even 'here at home' (p. 75).

Similar debates litter the history of *Othello* criticism. Few critics have been as damning as Rymer, and most consider *Othello* amongst Shakespeare's masterpieces, often above *Hamlet, King Lear* and *Macbeth*. Johnson found flaws in all of the latter plays, and praised *Othello* alone for its 'most exact and scrupulous regularity' (Vickers, 1974, p. 166). Coleridge thought *Othello* a superior play to *Lear* and *Hamlet*: in *Othello* 'the whole mature powers of his mind are displayed in admirable equilibrium' (Coleridge, 1835, p. 34). William Hazlitt also thought *Othello* the best of the tragedies: the pathos in *Lear* may be more overpowering, he wrote, but in *Othello* it is more natural, the play invites more sympathy than *Macbeth*, and compared to the 'remote' *Hamlet, Othello* is 'at once equally profound and affecting' (Hazlitt, 1818, p. 61). However, the point that divided Rymer and

Giddon also divided Coleridge and Hazlitt. Coleridge insisted that Othello could not be black: 'Othello must not be conceived of as a negro,' he wrote in 1822, 'but a high and chivalrous Moorish chief' (Coleridge, 1835, p. 33). Coleridge elaborated this point in his notes on *Othello*, where he argued that we should ignore isolated passages which describe Othello as black and use our common sense: 'as we are constituted, and most surely as an English audience was disposed in the beginning of the 17th century, it would be something monstrous to conceive this beautiful Venetian girl falling in love with a veritable negro'. He continues, 'It would argue a disproportionateness, a want of balance, in Desdemona, which Shakespeare does not appear in the least to have contemplated' (Coleridge, 1930, p. 47). Coleridge takes a similar view to Rymer, both are repulsed by the notion of Desdemona falling in love with a black man. Hazlitt, Coleridge's contemporary, took a different view. Writing about a production in which Kean played the part without blackface, he insisted that Othello 'was black' (quoted by Hankey, 2005, p. 38).

These early critics of *Othello*, though in some respects as varied as any of us in our readings, share a preoccupation with Othello's nobility and Desdemona's sexuality. Both are different ways of approaching the same questions: why does Othello believe Iago rather than Desdemona? And how can their love be capable of producing such horrific violence? As Hazlitt points out, Othello never seems to be a character in deep conflict. Rather, he moves in painful stages from the certainty of the noble warrior in Act I to the equally unstoppable murderer of Act V. Hazlitt calls this progression a 'movement of passion'. Othello does not argue with himself (or the audience) in the way that Macbeth and Iago do. Othello flips from sensuous passion to murderous rage in just one scene: 'in *Othello*, the doubtful conflict between contrary passions, though dreadful, continues only for a short time, and the chief interest is excited by the alternative ascendancy of different passions, the entire and unforeseen change from the fondest love and most unbounded confidence to the tortures of jealousy and the madness of hatred' (Hazlitt, 1818, p. 69). Each step of the way, Othello's immersion in his 'passions' is absolute, unyielding.

In the 20th century, F.R. Leavis advanced the critical understanding of this question by rejecting the view (put forward by A.C. Bradley) that the play is about the corruption of a 'nearly faultless hero' by 'the devilish cunning of Iago' (Leavis, 1952, p. 137). Leavis argued that Iago only has a hold over Othello because he exposes something that is already there: 'Iago's power . . . is that he represents something that is in Othello . . . the essential traitor is within the gates' (pp. 140–141). Leavis presents Othello as a self-dramatising man who creates an ideal version of himself as a noble hero which he is then tragically unable to live up to. We should no more trust Othello's words than Iago's: 'Othello's lack of self-knowledge is shown as humiliating and disastrous' (p. 147). T.S. Eliot likewise found little to admire in Othello, whom he described as 'a pathetic figure' looking to escape reality and dramatises himself to avoid confronting his situation (Eliot, 1927, p. 110).

Leavis's interpretation was immediately influential and underpinned Laurence Olivier's interpretation of the part. Olivier's extravagant, histrionic Othello bellowed Iago off the stage, and Leavis's Othello has had the same role in criticism – paving the way, if unintentionally, for the race-conscious focus of modern criticism. Leavis's core argument was later refashioned, and in effect remounted, for modern readers by Stephen Greenblatt. In *Renaissance Self-fashioning*, Greenblatt argues that Othello's identity 'depends upon a constant performance . . . of his story, a loss of his own origins, an embrace and perpetual reiteration of the norms of another culture' (Greenblatt, 1980, p. 245). Greenblatt takes forward Leavis's main insight, that Othello is not a blameless hero corrupted by a madman, but that he is in some way author of his own tragedy.

However, Leavis sidelined two questions which Rymer and Giddon confronted: Othello's race and Desdemona's sexuality. Of Othello's race, Leavis says little at all, in fact he dismisses as anachronistic the notion of what he calls 'colour prejudice' in the period. Othello displaces Desdemona entirely, even if Harold Bloom is correct that Leavis, along with Eliot, began a critical trend towards denigrating Othello's character and robbing him of his 'dignity and glory' (Bloom, 1998, p. 433). Modern criticism has seized on race and sexuality as the starting point for interpretation. Unexpectedly, criticism has returned to Rymer's obsessions with the 'black-amoor' and the potency of portraying miscegenation onstage. When a recent critic, Emily C. Bartels, argues that the drama's defining tension 'is the all-too likely prospect that a Moor *in* Venice could as well be a Moor *of* Venice' (Bartels, 2008, p. 159), we are returned to the point which enraged Rymer, for whom the notion of a 'Moor of Venice' was an absurd oxymoron. For modern critics, the same observation is the source of genuine critical interest. Since the late 1960s, discussion of these questions has accelerated to the point where any analysis is intimately bound up with contemporary attitudes to race and sexuality. For the remainder of this chapter, I shall consider in more detail critical approaches to Othello and his race, and to Desdemona and sexuality.

The Othello complex

The centrality of Othello to modern Shakespeare criticism is indicated by the cover of *Shakespeare and Race* (2000, edited by Catherine M. Alexander and Stanley Wells) which shows an RSC still of Willard White's Othello about to kiss Imogen Stubbs's Desdemona, whose mouth is open, her lips lasciviously pursed, ready to kiss (this is from Trevor Nunn's 1989 production for the RSC, which is discussed in Chapter 4). Othello has his hand around her neck in a way which foreshadows the play's turn from sexual desire to domestic violence. That these critics should choose Othello as the defining image of critical studies of Shakespeare and race is not surprising. Othello and race studies are intertwined in complex ways in modern critical discourse. Even so, the picture is a challenging one, not least because it makes white female sexuality a major part of the way in which the Shakespeare-race debate is developed. Othello looks like the racist stereotype of a black man for whom sexual desire hovers between sensuality and violence; Desdemona's pose seems to pander to male fear about the power of female sexual desire. Yet neither actor looks confined by these stereotypes, which they provocatively embrace with such conviction that any attempt to reduce them to centuries of fear and loathing fails. They are about to kiss, and in the history of modern Western race relations, a kiss between a black man and a white woman is loaded with cultural significance. The still embodies the key concerns which now drive critical response to the play: the politics of race, sexuality, miscegenation and identity.

In one of *Shakespeare and Race*'s keynote essays, Ania Loomba describes Shakespeare's period as 'a time which can be characterised as either the last period in history where ethnic identities could be understood as fluid, or as the first moment of the emergence of modern notions of "race" ' (Alexander and Wells, 2000, p. 203). *Othello* is an important play for race studies because it anticipates modern racism, particularly through characters like Iago whose vicious comments on Othello's skin colour pepper the play. However, *Othello* is not a modern play, and by historicising it, as Loomba does, critics are alive to the instabilities and contradictions which make up Othello's role in the play. This makes *Othello* a play less about race than racism. For Bartels, the word 'Moor' is (in its early modern context and in modern interpretations) an inherently unstable term which makes it a 'site where competing, always provisional axes of identity come into play, disrupting our ability, if not our desire, to assign the Moor a colour, religion, ethnicity or any homogonizing trait' (Bartels, 2008, p. 7). *Othello* both fulfils and evades racist stereotypes.

Although race in *Othello* today seems inescapable, critical studies in the question only began to emerge in the 1960s. In 1965, at the height of the civil rights movement's protests in America, Eldred D. Jones published a landmark study, *Othello's Countrymen: A Study of Africa in the Elizabethan and Jacobean Drama* (1965) which, for the first time, put Othello's race at the centre of an assessment of the play's historical significance, and asked important questions about how Shakespeare and his contemporaries conceptualised and directly experienced Africa. Along with later books by Elliot H. Tokson, Jones's work opened up a rich seam of critical possibilities which is still being mined. Jones challenged the conventional view that Shakespeare and his contemporaries had little direct experience of African Moors. However, Jones stopped short of making direct analogies with contemporary racial politics (Bartels, 2008, p. 10).

In the UK, G.K. Hunter published an important (albeit now very dated) essay which assessed the role of racism (or, as he calls it, 'colour prejudice') in the play. Hunter regarded Shakespeare's treatment of race as anachronistic and problematic for modern readers. However, he makes some unintentional assumptions about who reads and watches *Othello*. Shakespeare, he writes, 'has caught our over-easy assent to such assumptions in the grip of a guilt which associates us and our assent with the white man representative of such views in the play – Iago. Othello acquires the glamour of an innocent man whom we have wronged' (Hadfield, 2002, p. 68). Hunter was ahead of his time in noting the powerful sense of guilt and complicity which Shakespeare elicits from audiences. The play's depiction of race is really a negotiation – a very warped negotiation – between the play and the audience. Yet Hunter makes a very broad assumption about who 'we' are and how likely we are to have an 'over-easy assent' to racist views: he assumes 'we' are white.

The next generation of critics made no such assumptions, and in fact brought into critical view questions about the role of readers and audiences in negotiating the play's treatment of race. New historicist critics in particular have used Jones's work to explore the dynamic and evolving nature of race politics in the early modern period, and post-colonial critics have traced *Othello*'s paradoxical history of first being used to create colonial identities and then being appropriated by post-colonial theatre companies. For Thomas Cartelli, not only has '*Othello* . . . failed to unsettle or dislodge established racial stereotypes', it has also 'played a formative role in shaping them into what may well be termed the "Othello complex"'. Drawing on the work of Michael Neill, Cartelli goes on to describe this complex as a version of racial construction in which the 'assimilated savage' will, under duress, revert to his or her primitive condition (Cartelli, 1999, p. 123; Neill, 1989, p. 393). *Othello* cannot challenge this myth because the play is part of it. Othello's race is neither neutral nor contained within simplistic debates about whether Othello is African or Arabic. Loomba sees Othello's blackness as central to the play. In her reading, Othello is a black man trying to win acceptance in a white world. By becoming a General, he is an 'honorary white', and when he addresses the Venetians with long, elegant speeches, he attempts to 'speak better than any the language of his adoptive civilisation'. Desdemona is part of this strategy, she is a 'gate to white humanity'. However, under pressure, Othello also frequently resorts to exotic stories about his adventures, he 'oscillates between asserting his non-European glamour and denying his blackness'. This is a divide which can never be resolved. Like many post-colonial subjects caught between the competing pressures of assimilation and authenticity, Othello is 'hopelessly split' (Loomba, 1989, pp. 52–54).

Othello's divided racial identity has preoccupied some critics who agree with Dympna Callaghan's arresting observation that, as far as Shakespeare and Burbage were concerned, 'Othello was a white man.' Neill sees *Othello* as a play caught on the cusp of competing narratives of race which it invokes without committing to either one. Othello is 'far more fair than black', as the Duke says in 1.3, but by the play's end the Venetians regard Othello as a monster, a 'blacker devil' (5.2.129). Neill calls this a 'systematic blackening of the Moor' which starts with Roderigo's racist comments in Act I. In fact, writes Neill, 'Othello's blackness seems to be an almost casual effect of Iago's improvisatory malice and of Roderigo's and Brabantio's gullibility' (Neill, 1998, p. 373). *Othello* seems to be a racist play in that it depicts the failure of multiculturalism, but the behaviour of the Venetians at the end of the play, 'calls into question the sustainability of the racial scapegoating that Iago has brought about, forcing us to pay attention to a very different narrative – the one that ends . . . in a kiss that self-consciously proclaims an act of union'. That the play can be both racist and anti-racist at the same time is why *Othello* 'continues to torment us' (p. 374).

Camille Wells Slights questions the common critical interpretation of Othello's tragedy as a failure of assimilation. To accept this view would be to argue that his journey from being a military hero to murdering Desdemona is 'one of a black barbarian emerging from behind his civilized mask and reverting to his savage origins' (Slights, 1997, p. 384). In Slights's argument, Othello is not a stranger in Venice, on the contrary, he is Venice's most complete subject, the most Venetian of all Venetians. He is the 'Moor *of* Venice', Slights reminds us, and his self-fashioned identity is built entirely on the shared values of Venetian society. Like Neill and Loomba, Slights is alert to the play's contradictory manoeuvres between racism and non-racism: 'the play neither portrays nor evokes stable responses to Othello's blackness'. Racist language is counterbalanced with celebrations of Othello's skills and achievements: 'Othello's blackness and cultural displacement are correlative of, rather than contrasting with, his role as self-defined, autonomous citizen' (p. 386). Iago exploits Othello's Venetian values, warping them into an obsessive need for certainty. When the evidence of the handkerchief is presented to him, Othello becomes, like a slave, excluded from social order, so 'he kills Desdemona and himself in a desperate effort to regain connection with society through identification with ordered, free Venice' (p. 388).

Race and sexuality cross in the work of Janet Adelman, who plays with the notion that Othello's blackness contaminates Desdemona. In her reading, Othello sees his own blackness as a stain which is 'specifically associated with sexuality'. Adelman argues that Othello is wrapped up in a version of race that owes more to Iago's poisonous construction of blackness than to his own African identity. Adelman writes that 'Othello's experience of race as it comes to dominate his sense of himself as polluted and polluting, undeserving of Desdemona and hence quick to believe her unfaithful' (Adelman, 1997, p. 126). Iago in effect empties himself into the monster that he makes Othello into, so the poisoned version of race which Othello himself identifies with is ultimately one that belongs to Iago. In other words, blackness is a trope that overshadows all three principal characters.

Modern criticism has made huge advances in its understanding of how race operates in the play both culturally and thematically, and yet the play remains frustratingly elusive. Is Othello a white man's version of a black man, or a deeply realised and complex portrait of the post-colonial subject? Is *Othello* a racist play or a play about racism? Does Othello have a racial identity, or is it inscribed on him by Iago, Brabantio and Roderigo? *Othello*'s success as a play depends in part on the way it maintains this ambiguity without resolving any of these questions in a definitive way. This might torment critics like Neill, but Shakespeare's radical ambivalence about race gives *Othello* a compelling force rich in possibilities for contemporary performance.

Black ram and white ewe

Sasha Roberts calls *Othello* a tragedy 'of love' and groups it with *Romeo and Juliet* and *Antony and Cleopatra*. However, *Othello* immediately stands apart from those two plays. It is not called *Othello and Desdemona*, nor would the title be an apt one. All three plays are love stories which *should* go well, which we want to succeed, but all end in death. Only in *Othello* does one of the lovers kill the other, and only in *Othello* is the woman accused of being an adulteress and a whore by her lover with scant opportunity (only on her death bed) to understand the accusations and refute them. Juliet and Cleopatra know what kind of play they are in, and are acutely aware of the dangers of their affair. Unlike Juliet and Cleopatra, Desdemona is the 'object of sympathy, not disapproval' (Roberts, 2003, p. 119). As Gayle Greene puts it, 'the love that we see in this play seems inexorably linked to brutality' (Greene, 2004, p. 656).

Just as race is constructed in the play, so is gender and, as Greene argues, the play is composed of different constructions of women. Desdemona is the virtuous, prized daughter, then she is a betrayer of her family; she is Othello's passionate lover, then she is an adulteress. Brabantio's parting words to Othello, 'She has deceived her father, and may thee' (1.3.314), resound across the play and fatally undermine Othello's trust in Desdemona perhaps even more than anything that Iago says to him. Greene argues that Othello's language and attitudes to women make it possible for Iago to gull him into murder. Othello's words betray 'a suspicion of sexuality and the physical being of man and woman' which Iago easily exploits; his conviction that all women are faithless leads to a possessiveness which can only lead to death. Othello does not see Desdemona as a person, but as a subject for his own anxieties about women and sexuality: it is 'Othello's failure to see Desdemona as a person' that explains Iago's power over him (Greene, 2004, pp. 660–661). Celia R. Daileader does not even see *Othello* as primarily a play about race, but about 'a woman killed . . . for having sex'. Noting how few critics are ready to see *Othello* as a play about domestic violence, Daileader argues that more critical attention should be given to the play's treatment of transgressive sexuality (Daileader, 2005, p. 2). Greene echoes Daileader when she writes that '*Othello* is concerned, in action and theme, with men's misunderstanding of women' (Greene, 2004, p. 658).

This argument is echoed by Lisa Jardine, who sees Desdemona as a slandered woman trapped by Othello's public denunciation. Desdemona and other women are frequently defined by the male characters' lewd comments, most notably when Iago teases Desdemona in 2.1. By 4.2, Iago's comic innuendo has become recirculated through Othello's violent and public defamation of Desdemona's character (Jardine, 1996, p. 28). He calls her a strumpet in public, and then in private (but overheard by Emilia) a whore. All of the women in the play encounter a similar accusation: Emilia is thought to have slept with Othello, and Bianca's exact status (is she Cassio's mistress or prostitute?) is deliberately ambiguous. Once called whore, Jardine argues, Desdemona is irretrievably slandered: her 'two remaining scenes focus on her now supposedly culpable sexuality, culminating in her suffocation on her bed, in a state of undress – a whore's death for all her innocence' (p. 31). The critical study of gender inevitably coincides with, and sometimes conflicts

with, the study of race. For example, Carol Chillingotn Rutter has
no hesitation in acknowledging that *Othello* is a race 'narrative of
strangeness' but develops a study of *Othello* as a 'failed gossip text'
about 'truant housekeeping', as an alternative play which emerges
when Emilia's story is foregrounded (Rutter, 2000, p. 145). For Karen
Newman, femininity is a force which interrupts the play to become
'a counter-narrative to race'. The theme of mixed-race sexuality
seeps into the play's language, which is full of 'linked oppositions'
of 'black ram' and 'white ewe', 'fair' and 'black', 'angel' and 'devil'
(Newman, 1991, pp. 74–75). Male characters such as Iago are afraid
of Othello's sexual power, and merely use racist language to deni-
grate what they see as a 'different and monstrous' sexuality. Underlying this fear is a widely held early modern anxiety that black men
could contaminate white women with their blackness: 'the union
of Desdemona and Othello represents a sympathetic identification
between femininity and the monstrous that offers a potential subversive recognition of sexual and racial difference' (pp. 85–86). By
representing Desdemona as both virtuous and capable of transgressive sexual desire, the play challenges the orthodox view of women
and sex held by other characters in the play. The subversive force
of Othello and Desdemona's marriage is also discussed by Lara
Bovilsky, who cleverly draws out those aspects of Desdemona's character, and by Daileader, for whom the 'monstrous birth' that Iago
speaks refers to the birth of 'the inter-racial couple itself' (Daileader,
2005, p. 23).

Conclusion

Criticism has come a long way since Thomas Rymer inaugurated
Othello's critical tradition. Modern criticism has constantly returned
to the same questions as interest in the play's experimental exploration of tragic sexuality has become enmeshed in very contemporary and often political debates about race and gender. It is important
to contextualise *Othello*, to understand the play and Shakespeare as
products of their historical period; it is also important to recognise
how strange the play is when set against other plays from the period,
and how much it anticipates subsequent changes in society and culture. The contemporary fascination with the play's uncanny echoes

of present-day concerns demonstrates the extent to which *Othello* interacts with its context. The audience, and the reader, are essential parts of the way that the play works. Iago is our interlocutor, but that means that we are also part of the play, and as audiences have changed over the centuries, so has the play. As Ben Okri writes, 'If *Othello* is not a play about race, then its history has made it one' (Okri, 1988, p. 10). *Othello* is not a play which can or should be divorced from the present moment of its reading and performance.

Further Reading

I have used Jonathan Bate and Eric Rasmussen's edition of *Othello* throughout (Basingstoke: Palgrave, 2009).

I Text

E.A.J. Honigmann, *The Texts of 'Othello' and Shakespearian Revision* (London and New York: Routledge, 1996).

Scott McMillin (ed.), *The First Quarto of 'Othello'* (Cambridge: Cambridge University Press, 2001).

II Performance

Lynda E. Boose, 'Grossly Gaping Viewers and Jonathan Miller's *Othello*', in Lynde E. Boose and Richard Burt (eds), *Shakespeare, the Movie: Popularising the Plays on Film, TV, and Video* (London and New York: Routledge, 1997), pp. 190–201.

Martin Duberman, *Paul Robeson: A Biography* (New York: The New Press, 1995).

Mark W. Estrin (ed.), *Orson Welles: Interviews* (Jackson: University Press of Mississippi, 2002).

Julia Hankey, *Shakespeare in Production: Othello*, 2nd edn (Cambridge: Cambridge University Press, 2005).

Lisa Hopkins, '*Othello*. Adapted for Television by Andrew Davies', *Early Modern Literary Studies*, 8.1 (May, 2002), 11.1-4, available at http://purl.oclc.org/emls/08-1/othellorev.htm (accessed 3 February 2010).

James Earl Jones, *Othello* (London: Faber, 2003).

———— and Penelope Niven, *Voices and Silences* (New York: Scribner, 2002).

Laurence Olivier, *On Acting* (London: Sceptre, 1987).

Lois Potter, *Shakespeare in Performance: Othello* (Manchester: Manchester University Press, 2002).

Hugh Quarshie, *Second Thoughts About Othello* (Chipping Campden: Clouds Hill Printers, 1999).

Robert Speaight, *Shakespeare on the Stage* (London: Collins, 1973).

Janet Suzman, 'South Africa in *Othello*', in Jonathan Bate, Jill Levenson and Dieter Mehl (eds), *Shakespeare in the Twentieth Century: The Selected Proceedings of the International Shakespeare Association World Congress, Los Angeles, 1996* (Newark: University of Delaware Press, 1998), pp. 23–40.

Kenneth Tynan, *Othello: The National Theatre Production* (London: Stein & Day, 1967).

Virginia Mason Vaughan, *Performing Blackness on English Stages, 1500–1800* (Cambridge: Cambridge University Press, 2005).

Robert Weimann, *Shakespeare and the Popular Tradition: Studies in the Social Dimension of Dramatic Form and Function* (Baltimore: Johns Hopkins University Press, 1978).

Susan Willis, *The BBC Shakespeare Plays: Making the Televised Canon* (Chapel Hill: University of North Carolina Press, 1991).

III   Cultural Contexts

Janet Adelman, 'Iago's Alter Ego: Race as Projection in *Othello*', *Shakespeare Quarterly*, Vol. 48, No. 2 (Summer, 1997), pp. 125–144.

Catherine M. Alexander and Stanley Wells (eds), *Shakespeare and Race* (Cambridge: Cambridge University Press, 2000).

Emily C. Bartels, *Speaking of the Moor: From Alcazar to Othello* (Philadelphia: University of Pennsylvania Press, 2008).

Lara Bovilsky, *Barbarous Play: Race on the English Renaissance Stage* (Minneapolis: University of Minnesota Press, 2008).

Dympna Callaghan, *Shakespeare Without Women: Representing Gender and Race on the Renaissance Stage* (London and New York: Routledge, 2000).

Thomas Cartelli, *Repositioning Shakespeare: National Formations, Postcolonial Appropriations* (London and New York: Routledge, 1999).

Mary Ellen Cacheado (ed.), *Lust's Dominion, or the Lascivious Queen* (Hosted by *Early Modern Literary Studies*, 2005), available at http://extra.shu.sac.uk/emls/iemls/renplays/lustsdominion.htm (accessed 3 March 2010).

Celia R. Daileader, *Racism, Misogyny, and the Othello Myth: Inter-racial Couples from Shakespeare to Spike Lee* (Cambridge: Cambridge University Press, 2005).

Gayle Greene, ' "This that you call love": Sexual and Social Tragedy in *Othello*', *Journal of Women's Studies in Literature* Vol. 1, No. 1 (Winter 1979), pp. 16–32, reproduced in Russ MacDonald (ed.), *Shakespeare: An Anthology of Criticism and Theory, 1945–2000* (Oxford: Blackwell, 2004), pp. 655–668.

Kim Hall, '*Othello* and the Problem of Blackness', in Richard Dutton and Jean Howard (eds), *A Companion to Shakespeare's Works: The Tragedies* (Oxford: Blackwell, 2003), pp. 357–374.

G.K. Hunter, 'Othello and Colour Prejudice', *Proceedings of the British Academy*, LIII (1967), pp. 139–163, reproduced in Hadfield (2002), pp. 66–74.

Lisa Jardine, *Reading Shakespeare Historically* (London and New York: Routledge, 1996).

Eldred D. Jones, *Othello's Countrymen: A Study of Africa in the Elizabethan and Jacobean Drama* (Oxford: Oxford University Press, 1965).

Ania Loomba, *Gender, Race, Renaissance Drama* (Manchester: Manchester University Press, 1989).

Eric Lott, *Love and Theft: Blackface Minstrelsy and the American Working Class* (Oxford: Oxford University Press, 1995).

Michael Neill, 'Unproper Beds: Race, Adultery, and the Hideous in Othello', *Shakespeare Quarterly*, Vol. 40, No. 4 (Winter, 1989), pp. 383–412.

——— ' "Mulattos," "Blacks," "and Indian Moors": *Othello* and Early Modern Constructions of Human Difference', *Shakespeare Quarterly*, Vol. 49, No. 4 (Winter, 1998), pp. 361–374.

Karen Newman, *Fashioning Feminity and English Renaissance Drama* (Chicago: University of Chicago Press, 1991).

Ben Okri, 'Leaping out of Shakespeare's Terror: Five Meditations on *Othello*', in Kwesi Owusu (ed.), *Storms of the Heart* (London: Camden Press, 1988), pp. 9–18.

Sasha Roberts, 'Reading Shakespeare's Tragedies of Love: *Romeo and Juliet*, *Othello*, and *Antony and Cleopatra* in Early Modern England', in Richard Dutton and Jean Howard (eds), *A Companion* to *Shakespeare's Works: The Tragedies* (Oxford: Blackwell, 2003), pp. 108–133.

Carol Chillington Rutter, *Enter the Body: Women and Representation on Shakespeare's Stage* (London and New York: Routledge, 2000).

Elliot H. Tokson, *The Popular Image of the Black Man in English Drama, 1550–1688* (Boston: G.K. Hall, 1982).

Ayanna Thompson, 'The Blackfaced Bard: Returning to Shakespeare or Leaving Him?', *Shakespeare Bulletin*, Vol. 27, No. 3 (Fall, 2009), pp. 437–456.

James Walvin, *The Black Presence: A Documentary History of the Negro in England, 1550–1860* (New York: Schocken Book, 1971).

IV Critical Approaches

Harold Bloom, *Shakespeare: The Invention of the Human* (New York: Riverhead Books, 1998).

A.C. Bradley, *Shakespearean Tragedy* (London: Macmillan, 1904).

Pamela Allan Brown, '*Othello* Italicised: Xenophobia and the Erosion of Tragedy', in Michele Marrapodi (ed.), *Shakespeare, Italy, and Intertextuality* (Manchester: Manchester University Press, 2004), pp. 145–157.

Samuel Taylor Coleridge, *Specimens of the Table Talk of the Late Samuel Taylor Coleridge*, Vol. 1 (New York: Harper, 1835).

——— *Coleridge's Shakespearean Criticism*, Vol. 1, Thomas Middleton Raysor (ed.) (Cambridge: Harvard University Press, 1930).

T.S. Eliot, *Shakespeare and the Stoicism of Seneca* (Oxford: Shakespeare Association Papers, 1927).

Stephen Greenblatt, *Renaissance Self-fashioning: From More to Shakespeare* (Chicago: University of Chicago Press, 1980).

Andrew Hadfield (ed.), *A Routledge Literary Sourcebook on William Shakespeare's 'Othello'* (London and New York: Routledge, 2002).

William Hazlitt, *Characters of Shakespeare's Plays* (Boston: Wells and Lilly, 1818).

F.R. Leavis, 'Diabolic Intellect and the Noble Hero', *Scrutiny*, Vol. 6 (1937), pp. 259–283, reproduced in F.R. Leavis, *The Common Pursuit* (London: Chatto & Windus, 1952), pp. 136–159.

Edward Pechter, *Othello and Interpretative Traditions* (Iowa: University of Iowa Press, 1999).

Camille Wells Slights, 'Slaves and Subjects in *Othello*', *Shakespeare Quarterly*, Vol. 48, No. 4 (Winter, 1997), pp. 377–390.

Virginia Mason Vaughan, *Othello: A Contextual History* (Cambridge: Cambridge University Press, 1994).

Brian Vickers (ed.), *William Shakespeare: The Critical Heritage 1693–1733* (London and New York: Routledge, 1974).

Index